C000231914

DASHERS

KATIE'S LARDER

MORE DISHES WITH Dashers

COOKING FOR FRIENDS

Katie Dashwood

Peto Publishing

First Published in the UK in 2017
Peto Publishing

British Library Cataloguing-in-Publication Data
A catalogue record for this book
is available from the British Library

ISBN 9781999895600

The information in this book is true and complete to the best of our knowledge.

Designed and typeset by Simon Vowles
Printed in the UK and Creative by SpiffingCovers.com
Previous Publication: Dishes with Dashers

For Nick, MVVBB

Contents

Acknowledgements

To Nick, without whom I would never have pushed myself to get this book printed and out onto the shelves. To this end, he has put up with me closeted in my study for hours on end and, as a result, has eaten lunches and suppers at some fairly random times of the day and night.

To Simon Vowles - who possesses the patience of a Saint, and an unflappable one at that. He has worked ceaselessly to organise the layout, design and illustrations throughout the book so that it was ready to send to the printers. Without his help, I would still be shuffling through a pile of dishevelled pages.

To Emma Storey - as one who understands, loves and cooks food with great flair - her meticulous editing of the receipts within have been a calming, organised and practical godsend. She has also endured a great deal of receipt testing and tasting.

To Charlie Sainsbury-Plaice - friend and photographer. Charlie is well known for his extraordinary skills behind a camera. What makes his talents even more special is his deep-rooted knowledge of the countryside and his subjects.

To those chefs and professional cooks whose creations and writings have inspired and widened my culinary knowledge and instilled in me an on-going desire to produce honest food. And to all my friends who have so liberally entertained me for years, unhesitatingly sharing their culinary secrets and receipts with me. It is their generosity which has made food fun for me. Superheroes, each and every one of you!

Introduction

Whilst working on ***'More Dishes With Dashers'*** (albeit over a less than speedy gestation period!), there appears to have been a shift in cooking which focuses on simplified techniques rather than being a slave to the kitchen. Not only do we want to spend less time at the stove, but we demand both revered classics leaning on nostalgia as well as dishes that ignite the senses in terms of texture, taste and colour - inspired by vibrant, modern-day food trends.

Over-complicated receipts and thumbing through a plethora of cookbooks can take the joy out of rustling up something tasty every day. You can count on ***'More Dishes With Dashers'*** as the 'go-to' bible which covers a range of easy-to-follow and delectable suggestions covering a spectrum of dishes from elegant game to sensational salads; make-ahead canapés to warming puddings and even a cocktail bar for those looking to make the party rock. You'll find inspirations for just about any occasion; be it a speedy no-cook little number after a demanding day or a make-ahead something so that you can relax when giving parties whilst surprising your guests with traditional and unique dishes to produce show-stopping results.

Life for me has changed from entertaining solo in my own home with dash and panache to now being very happily married to Nick where there is now the matter of putting both lunch and supper on the table daily without too much faff. Old faithfuls - roast chicken, four-cheese macaroni, shepherd's pie - make regular appearances and lengthy receipts are now eschewed in favour of something quicker yet just as, if not more, tasty. That said, cooking for our friends plays an important part in our lives - I have always believed that food is for loving, giving and sharing and I certainly revel in the fact that many of the receipts within these pages are fantastic 'Get-Ahead' wonders such as Potted Shrimps, Thai Shitake Pheasant and Salted Crème Caramel. After all, entertaining is about enjoying the company of one's guests, rather than stressing over steaming pots and pans. Our parties at Grey Walls are a joint effort and definitely a do-it-ourselves show designed for ease.

'We do not eat alone, but in families or sets of friends; and the table is the best centre of friendships'.

CHARLES W. ELLIOT, THE HAPPY LIFE 1896

Receipts are often best shared with a story, rather than a picture. It gives each one its poetry and each time the tale is told, the lineage and life of the dish is revitalised. A number of dishes are collected from kind friends after savouring such delights in their company as well as from those culinary establishments whose cooking, thanks to their unfailingly popular classics, has stood the test of time. Rosie Abel-Smith's Sweet Potato, Cucumber & Mint Soup is one such example that exudes charm and vitality, part of the soup collection to warm and lighten the soul. Rowley Leigh's Parmesan Custards that were heavenly favourites at Le Café Anglais are divulged here, unveiling a revived appreciation for such established classics.

Of course, the accent on what does arrive at the table should always rely on the best and most carefully selected seasonal ingredients. We live in an age where strawberries, raspberries, asparagus and so many other foods are available 365 days of the year, flown in from all over the World. Produce is at its best at a certain time of the year not only for taste and flavour but also as a means of supporting the agricultural, fishing and farming industries continuously. Stick to seasonality and you will reap the rewards of these characteristics that will make your dishes glow.

When it comes to ovens, I have always been an Aga-holic. This iconic work of iron warms the house, dries wet clothes and acts as a magnet for our dogs whose beds are firmly placed right up against it. (They are trained to budge when I need to open the doors!). My previous trusty two door Aga might well have been regarded as something of a museum piece with a mind of its own when deciding what temperature it wanted to be. It was a lesson well learnt to understand how to manage this and how quickly I came to appreciate that a little organisation and juggling is all that is really needed. By way of contrast, I now feel I am living in the New Age with an electric Aga but I shall always be thankful to my old Aga which would have won a prize for rust, and for teaching me the rudiments of coping!

Happy reading, happy cooking and happy eating!

■ This symbol represents a 'Get-Ahead' receipt

■ All serve 4 persons unless otherwise stated. The chapters on Canapés, Cocktails, Bits & Bobs and The Larder being obvious exceptions.

■ Measurements and quantities are given in both Metric and Imperial. It is advisable to work through a receipt using one or other measurement and not to mix the two.

■ A glass (of something) generally refers to around 110ml (4 fl oz).

■ Seasoning refers to sea salt - Maldon is my first choice - and either whole black or white peppercorns, freshly ground from a mill.

■ Butter is unsalted. Sugars are unrefined.

■ Chicken stock is homemade unless otherwise specified. Tubs of fresh stock or stock cubes may be substituted, although the resultant taste may differ and pay heed, they are often over-salted.

■ Herbs are fresh, unless otherwise stated.

■ Eggs are always fresh, free-range and large sized.

■ Dairy products are always the full-fat variety.

■ Olive oil is extra virgin, unless otherwise stated.

■ Meat comes from my butcher - Lambourne's in Stow-on-the-Wold and is unfailingly locally sourced. Bob and his team always advise me what is best, its provenance and, for how long each piece of meat has been hung. Furthermore, they will cut, trim, bone etc to my own specifications and will provide me with a bag of bones - for the stockpot and sauces.

■ Likewise, fish comes from my fishmongers - Severn & Wye Smokery. Once again, the team is highly knowledgeable and know how best to cook every type of fish they sell. Similarly, they will prepare what you have chosen - their skills at skinning and boning will save hours at home.

Soups

Soup – the word has such soothing connotations and there are times when nothing fits the bill quite like a bowl of liquid loveliness as the ultimate comfort dish. Be it a clear broth or a hearty 'stand up spoon' affair, it is classic feel-better food - nourishing and healthy. Whether one eats, drinks or merely sups (sips, even!) soup is a subject open to endless debate but I am really not bothered preferring, rather, just to concentrate on its sheer goodness and flavours.

PEA AND BASIL

A departure from the standard Pea and Mint duo, this verdant green alternative is equally fresh and vibrant. I often finish it off by floating a blob of pesto on the surface. Serve steaming in its tureen or chill it for hot summer days (and nights).

- Tbsp olive oil
- Onion, peeled and finely diced
- 500g / 1 lb frozen petit pois
- Handful each basil and mint leaves
- Pinch of white sugar
- Tsp sea salt
- 250g / 9 oz mascarpone or crème fraîche
- Pea shoots (available from good supermarkets or hedgerows)

Heat the oil in a saucepan, add the onion and sauté gently until soft and translucent. Add ⅔ of the peas, 600ml / just over 1 pint of water, half the mint and basil leaves, the sugar and salt. Bring to the boil then simmer for 20 minutes or until the peas are tender. Put the soup into a blender in batches or whizz with an electric hand stick, adding the remaining peas and herbs. Adjust the seasoning as necessary and run down with a little water to the required consistency. Serve either chilled or reheated. Garnish each bowl with a teaspoon of mascarpone and a few sprigs of pea shoots.

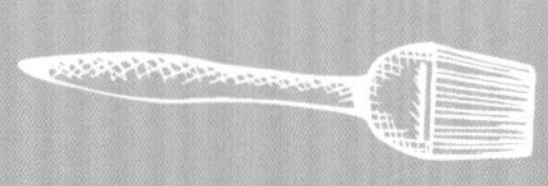

Tips FROM THE SINK

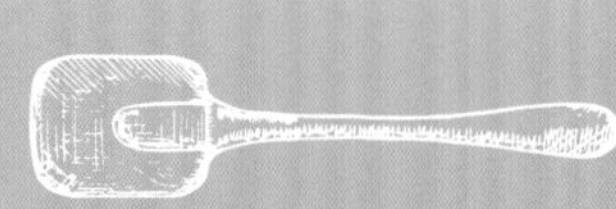

- By adding the remainder of the peas at the end, this ensures the soup is really fresh and green.
- If the soup is left thicker, use it as a purée to go with fish and poultry or, better still, to stir through a risotto.

LEEK, PEA AND SMOKED BACON

The addition of smoked bacon gives this oomph and depth of flavour.

- Onion, peeled and finely diced
- Splash olive oil
- 3 rashers smoked bacon, roughly chopped
- 4 medium leeks, white parts only, cleaned and diced
- 375g / 12 oz frozen garden peas or petit pois
- 600 ml / 1 pint chicken stock
- Seasoning

Cook the onion in the oil until soft and translucent then add the bacon and fry off until crisp but not burnt. Throw in the leeks and peas, pour in the stock and simmer gently for 20 minutes or so until the vegetables are cooked. Partially blend so that it is still quite chunky and season according to taste. Excellent with the Cheese Scones (page 168).

LIZ'S COURGETTE AND MINT

This receipt was given to me by Liz Bowden who has often assisted me during my cooking demos. Having trained as a nurse she is super organised and lays out all my utensils in neat rows as if they were scalpels in a surgeon's operating theatre. This is a brilliant way of dealing with that glut of courgettes and especially good served chilled. It can, of course, be made a couple of days in advance – helpful for every busy cook and which of us aren't?

- Medium onion, peeled and finely diced
- Litre / 2 pints chicken or vegetable stock
- 500 - 750g / 1- 1 ½ lbs courgettes, topped and tailed, roughly sliced
- 200g / 7 oz cream cheese
- Seasoning
- Handful fresh mint leaves, torn

Put the onion into a saucepan with the stock cube and add a little boiling water to cover. Cover the pan with a lid and cook the onion gently to soften, (7 - 10 minutes) stirring from time and time and making sure there is enough liquid so that it doesn't 'catch' and burn. Next, add the courgettes and the rest of the water, replace the lid and cook for a further 12 -15 minutes until the vegetables are done. Remove from the heat and add

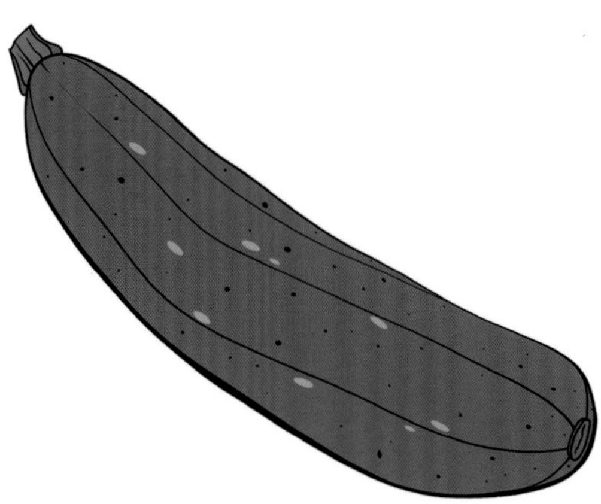

the cream cheese, either in a food processor or with an electric hand stick until smooth, throwing in the mint leaves whilst the machine is running. Season to taste – remember that commercial stock cubes (if using these) can be quite salty so don't get too carried away! If too thick, thin down with cold water then cover and leave to cool. This is excellent served cold (in which case also chill the bowls in the fridge beforehand) or reheated. Garnish the top of each one with a sprig of fresh mint.

BUTTERNUT, HONEY AND SAGE WITH CHESTNUTS

A classy warmer, good for autumnal days and Bonfire nights.

- Medium butternut, peeled, seeded and roughly chopped
- 50g / 2 oz butter
- Litre / 2 pints chicken or vegetable stock
- Leaves from one sprig of sage, finely chopped
- Dollop of clear honey
- Tbsp lemon juice
- Seasoning
- Double cream
- Handful vacuum-sealed chestnuts

Simply melt the butter in a saucepan then add the butternut and sage, honey and lemon juice together with a ladle or two of the stock. Cover with a lid and cook until soft. Add more stock and the cream (to colour), purée and season.

To serve, simply pan fry a handful of chestnuts, roughly chopped, in a little butter until crunchy and scatter over the surface of the soup.

OLD-FASHIONED TOMATO

Although I am a self-confessed Heinz addict, especially once doctored with Worcester sauce and a tot of sherry and preferably poured piping hot from a thermos – I am almost as fond of this 'oldie-worldly' no-cook soup, which has been a treasured receipt of Liz Acland's family for generations. Liz first introduced me to this pale, interesting and, I think, deliciously luxurious secret after one of our many gardening forays. It was the perfect pick-me-up after an extensive day with James Bolton's Border Lines Garden Tours looking at fabulous gardens, all mouth-watering in horticultural terms, in the West Country.

- 1.5 kg / 3 lbs ripe tomatoes
- 1 ½ tbsp sugar
- 3 tsp salt
- ¾ tsp onion juice
- Zest of ½ lemon
- 150ml / ¼ pint double cream
- 3 slices cooked ham, neatly diced
- Cucumber flesh, finely chopped
- Parsley, finely chopped

Purée the tomatoes in a blender and sieve. Chill thoroughly. Just before serving add sugar, salt, onion juice and the lemon zest. Stir well and add the cream, ham and cucumber. Sprinkle over the parsley before serving.

Tips FROM THE SINK

- To make onion juice, grate an onion and collect juice.

Soups

NETTLE & WILD GARLIC

Spring brings with it a profusion of wild plants and weeds, many of which are delicious for eating. Foraging for food has always been high on my list of priorities. There is something so pleasing about gathering ingredients from the hedgerows and eating for free. Rewarding, also, to transform some seemingly mundane ingredient into something subtle yet flavoursome. It was chef and restaurateur Bruce Poole whose wild garlic soup I first tasted and realised just how good it is. Bruce heads up the excellent trio of Chez Bruce, La Trompette and The Glasshouse. The first of these, based in Wandsworth, was my local 'go-to-for-treats' eatery when I lived in London and I still visit on special occasions. You need to be ready to make this when the nettles first start shooting and are young and tender.

- 100g / 4 oz butter
- Onion, peeled and chopped
- 2 large potatoes (such as Desirée), peeled and diced
- Leek, white part only, cleaned and diced
- 400g / 14 oz (or large carrier bag!) young nettles, leaves only
- 250g / 8 oz wild garlic leaves, plus a few flowers for decoration
- 850ml / 1 ½ pints chicken or vegetable stock
- Seasoning
- Freshly grated nutmeg
- Squeeze lemon juice
- Crème fraîche, to taste

Melt the butter in a saucepan then add the onion and leek and cook to soften for 10 minutes or so before adding the potatoes. Pour in the stock and continue cooking until the potatoes are done then bring to the boil, plunge in the nettles and wild garlic leaves and blanche just until they collapse (rather like cooking spinach). Do not continue to boil or the soup will turn a dirty brown and look most unappetising. Purée in either a blender or using an electric stick and season. Pass through a sieve, return to the pan and reheat before seasoning, then add in the nutmeg and lemon juice and whisk in some crème fraîche to finish. Serve hot with a blob of crème fraiche or creamy goats cheese on each bowl of soup.

SWEET POTATO, CUCUMBER AND MINT

Rosie Abel-Smith is a famous and very gifted garden designer and plants-person who lives her life at 100 mph rushing all over England creating the most outstanding gardens. I always love going to have lunch and supper with her and her husband Robert. Their house, buried deep in the Slad Valley, has a romance of its own, and is a hidden gem. There's also the chance to walk round her own magical garden. The food she brings to the table appears without so much as a whisper of effort and she is also a whizz at coming up with something new and innovative - such as this soup.

- Onion, peeled and finely diced
- Generous bunch fresh mint
- Small sweet potato, peeled and chopped
- Large cucumber, peeled and chopped
- Litre / 2 pints chicken stock
- Seasoning

Put a couple of ladles of stock into a saucepan and add the onion. Roughly strip the mint leaves from the stalks. Keep the leaves to one side and plunge the stalks into the pan. After 5 minutes, add the potato and cucumber and cook until soft adding more liquid as required. Add most of the mint leaves and purée until completely smooth. Season and serve hot or chilled, sprinkling over the remaining mint.

Tips FROM THE SINK

- In order to hold its colour, put the soup once made into a container in an ice bath so that it chills as quickly as possible.

GOLDEN BEETROOT AND SWEET POTATO

Perhaps more accurately this should simply be called 'Storey's Soup'. My neighbours Mike and Angie were without electricity (yet another power cut) so I suggested an impromptu lunch along with heat and light then realised the cupboards and fridge were pretty bare. So much for my largesse! Four golden beetroot, one sweet potato, a tin of consommé, a bottle of Big Tom and a dash of double cream later ...

- 4 golden beetroot, peeled and chopped
- Onion, peeled and finely diced
- Tin consommé soup
- Large sweet potato, peeled and diced
- 300ml / ½ pint tomato juice (I use Big Tom)
- Seasoning
- Generous pinch cayenne pepper
- Dash of double cream

Start by cutting the beets into evenly sized pieces and place these in a large pan then cover with cold water. Add salt and bring to the boil, cover with a lid and cook for approx 25 – 30 mins until soft. Remove from the heat and stand aside. Next, using another pan, pour in half the consommé soup, add the onion and cover with a lid and cook over a medium heat until the onion is soft. To this, add the strained beetroot, remaining consommé, tomato juice, seasonings and double cream. Blend and serve.

AVOCADO & LIME

One from Morocco, enjoyed with Martin and Anne Summers.

- 2 ripe avocados, peeled, stone and chopped
- 200g / 7 oz natural yoghurt
- Juice of 2 limes
- 435ml / ¾ pint vegetable stock
- Seasoning

Blend all together, adding a little cold water if too thick. Chill to serve.

GAZPACHO

Another from the Moroccan kitchens - this time courtesy of Alex Peto's cook and housekeeper Zhara. What is particularly pleasing about this version is the omission of green peppers which can have that 'repeat' effect. I also like its silky smoothness for sophistication.

- 4 ripe tomatoes, chopped
- Red pepper, seeded and chopped
- Yellow pepper, seeded and chopped
- ½ cucumber, peeled and diced
- Onion, peeled and chopped
- 2 garlic cloves, peeled and minced
- Tbsp tomato concentrate
- Tbsp capers, drained
- Tbsp vinegar
- Handful mint leaves
- 2 tbsp lemon juice
- 3 tbsp olive oil
- Seasoning
- Avocado, to garnish
- Chives

Blend everything together, bar the avocado and chives, in the food processor to combine. Pass through a sieve, check seasoning, then chill thoroughly until required. To serve, scatter chopped pieces of avocado over the top of each bowl and sprinkle over snipped chives.

Salads

Salads now scale celebrity status fame in everyday cuisine, be they something one has rustled up to enjoy at home or those which the greatest chefs create for their knock-out menus. Thankfully, images of yesteryear attempts are long forgotten. Instead, colourful plates of healthy and enticing ingredients, artfully yet easily assembled, radiate sunshine and vitamin D! And the plus point is that many of these don't necessarily even involve any actual cooking. Now you're talking.

PRAWN, CHICKPEA, PESTO, BLACK OLIVE AND SUN-BLUSH TOMATOES

- Tin chickpeas, drained and rinsed through with cold water
- 250g / 8 oz cooked cold-water shelled prawns
- 2 tbsp black olives, pitted
- Jar sun-blush tomatoes, drained
- Tub of pesto - fresh readymade is fine
- Olive oil

No more than a quick assembly job. Simply put the chickpeas in a bowl, add the prawns, olives and tomatoes. Run the pesto down to a thinner consistency with some olive oil and drizzle over everything.

TOMATO, RED PEPPER AND RED ONION SALAD

I love this dish with either griddled chicken, poached salmon or smoked fish such as mackerel.

- 2 roasted red peppers (page 228)
- Red onion, peeled and very thinly sliced
- 2 tbsp red wine vinegar
- Freshly ground sea salt
- 3 – 4 flavoursome ripe tomatoes, preferably vine, skinned (page 228)
- Pinch sugar
- Seasoning
- Handful fresh marjoram or oregano leaves, chopped

Heat the oven to 190 C. Cut the roasted and seeded red peppers into fine strips. Boil a kettle and put the onion slices in a sieve then pour over the boiling water. This removes any traces of acidity and rawness. Drain thoroughly then put into a bowl with the red wine vinegar and salt and set aside. Next, thinly sliced the skinned tomatoes and spread out in a single layer and sprinkle sparingly with the sugar as this brings out their natural sweetness. Remove the onions from the bowl and place together with the red ingredients in a shallow dish or onto a plate with a bit of a lip, season and sprinkle over the herbs.

BURRATA, GREEN BEANS & SERRANO HAM

Burrata is a fresh Italian cheese made from mozzarella and cream - king amongst its kin.

- 250g / 8 oz fine French beans
- 250g / 8 oz shelled broad beans
- 200g / 7 oz burrata, drained
- 75g / 3 oz serrano ham, torn into bits

Dressing:

- 20 basil leaves torn, plus a few extra left whole
- Tbsp sherry vinegar
- 3 tbsp olive oil
- Garlic clove, crushed
- Pinch caster sugar
- Seasoning

For the dressing, whizz the ingredients together thoroughly in the bowl of a food processor.

Top and tail the French beans and cook, together with the broad beans, in a pan of rapidly boiling salted water until just 'al dente'. Drain and refresh under cold running water to still the cooking and help retain their colour. Remove the skins from the broad beans and mix together in a bowl with the French beans then dot around the pieces of ham. Using a pair of scissors, chop up the burrata and scatter over the top. Scatter with the remaining whole basil leaves, toss with the dressing and serve.

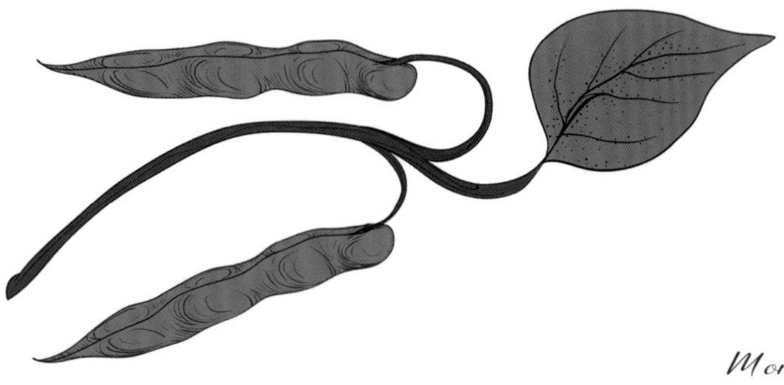

PANZANELLA SALAD
(SERVES 6 - 8)

This salad may well have started its life in modest Italian trattorias but now it is to be found everywhere. Everyone has their own interpretation as to what its components should be and mine makes no claim to be authentic. Do not worry if you do not have all the ingredients listed here to hand - this can be something of a mix and match compilation. The true essence of a good Panzanella lies in getting the bread dry enough so that it will not become soggy and in sourcing the sweetest and most fragrant tomatoes. It should be piled up high on a white serving or meat dish which will show off the vibrant colours. Make it in some volume as everyone is sure to devour second helpings. It really is the perfect way in which to start a leisurely summer's day lunch.

- Good ripe tomatoes
- Cherry tomatoes
- Sun-dried tomatoes, drained
- Radishes, trimmed and thinly sliced
- Cucumber, peeled, seeded and finely chopped
- Roasted red and yellow peppers (page 228)
- Handful of capers
- Spring onions, white part only, trimmed and thinly chopped
- Red onion, peeled and finely sliced
- Garlic cloves to taste, pounded to a paste with sea salt
- Feta
- A large 2-day-old loaf of ciabatta or country-style white bread
- Black olives, pitted
- Tin anchovy fillets
- Basil leaves, torn
- Flat-leaf parsley leaves, chopped
- Seasoning
- Olive oil
- Red wine vinegar

Remove the crusts from the bread, cut into small cubes and mix with the garlic. Place on a baking tray and toast lightly so that they do not take on any colour.

Scatter the tomatoes, both fresh and sun-dried, over the base of the platter then add radishes, cucumber, the roasted peppers cut into strips, the capers, onions, feta, olives, anchovy fillets and scatter on the herbs. Season and drizzle with finest olive oil and some red wine vinegar.

PINEAPPLE, RED ONION, CHILLI, LIME AND CORIANDER

Zingy and vibrant, this adds piquancy to a platter of cold meats.

- Ripe pineapple, skin and core removed, cut into neat chunks
- ½ red onion, peeled and thinly sliced
- Small red chilli, finely chopped, seeds removed
- Zest and juice of a lime
- Handful of coriander leaves, finely chopped
- Olive oil
- Seasoning

Mix all together and pile into a bowl to serve.

PURPLE SALAD

Shades of purple abound throughout this book and those who know me are well aware of my penchant for this regal colour; so it seems only fitting that a salad with such overtones this should feature amongst the pages. It looks as pretty as a picture on the plate too.

Call it chicory or endive, its tangy and slightly bitter taste brings a bit of zip and zing to any salad.

- Bunch fresh beetroot, washed and trimmed
- 2 - 3 garlic cloves, unpeeled
- Olive oil and balsamic vinegar
- 3 - 4 heads red chicory, leaves separated
- Small head of radicchio, trimmed
- Snippets of bacon or shards of Parma ham, cooked
- 4 ripe figs, topped, tailed and quartered
- Handful walnuts or pecan nuts, toasted

Preheat the oven to 190 C. Chop the beetroot into bite-sized pieces and, if the leaves are really fresh, wash and dry these and set aside to go into the salad. Place the beets on a double sheet of foil, cut each garlic clove into a few slivers and scatter over, then add a good slug of olive oil, a few shakes of balsamic vinegar, season generously and parcel up loosely and place in the oven. Cook for an hour or so, until soft.

On a large platter or meat dish, arrange the chicory and radicchio leaves, dot over the cooked beetroot and juices, then add the bacon / Parma ham, figs and nuts.

- Add thin slices of Manchego cheese or serve with my Parmesan Crisps (page 170).

BOXING DAY SALAD
(SERVES 5 - 6)

I can't think of anyone in the mood to spend hours in the kitchen on Boxing Day exhausted, as everyone is, from the excesses and efforts of the previous day. Christmas, after all, is full-on but St Stephen's Day is a far more relaxed affair and, for my money, far more enjoyable. There is cold turkey, a glistening great ham, smoked salmon, the remains of the Christmas pudding, Stilton and so on - hence lunch really calls for minimal culinary skills. Just slip some potatoes - skewered then slathered in olive oil and sea salt - into the oven to bake; assemble this blast from the past and the feast is on the table.

- Head of celery with leaves
- 2 ripe avocados, peeled, stoned and sliced
- 4 - 5 good flavoursome tomatoes, skinned (page 228)
- Vinaigrette (see page 211)
- Seasoning

Trim up the celery and strip away any stringy looking parts to the stalks. Chop crossways into neat little discs and toss into a dish or bowl. Chop the leaves finely and set to one side. To the celery, add the avocado. Thinly slice the tomatoes. Combine with the celery and avocados then add the dressing, season and leave to stand for an hour or so. Just before serving, sprinkle over the celery leaves.

BLOOD ORANGE SALAD

This smacks of Sicily, home of the blood orange. The real joy of this is the rich, deep red of the fruits so buy extra as not every individual orange is necessarily as 'blooded' inside as others and you really do want the darkest ones here.

- Red onion, peeled and halved, cut into thin crescents
- 8 blood oranges
- Tbsp fresh oregano or marjoram leaves
- Small packet pomegranate seeds (optional)
- 3 tbsp olive oil
- Freshly ground black pepper

Pile the onion slices into a sieve and rinse through with a kettle of boiling water to remove any hint of astringency. Rinse in cold water and pat dry on kitchen paper. Peel the oranges, taking care to remove the pith, and slice crossways into pinwheel rounds. Arrange the slices on a plate or shallow dish - white is the best - scatter over the radishes and onion, some oregano or marjoram leaves, the pomegranate seeds (if using) and season. Drizzle with oil just before bringing to the table.

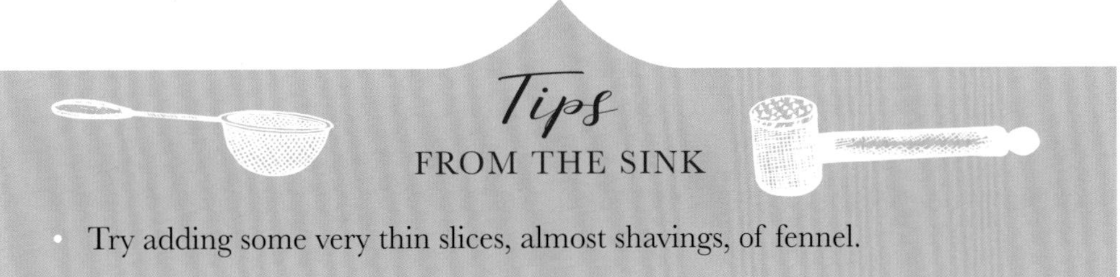

- Try adding some very thin slices, almost shavings, of fennel.

WINTER SALAD

Emma Storey first introduced me to this deliciously crunchy creation which goes particularly well with meaty terrines or cold ham. You can vary the ingredients too – try including carrot or celeriac.

- ¼ red cabbage, very finely sliced
- Apple, cored and cut into slivers
- Fennel bulb, thinly sliced, reserving feathery leaves
- 3 celery sticks, de-stringed and finely chopped
- Small red onion, peeled and thinly sliced
- Red chicory, thinly sliced
- 75g / 3 oz walnuts, dry toasted
- Good squeeze lemon juice

Dressing:

- 3 tbsp crème fraîche
- Splash red wine vinegar
- Tbsp wholegrain mustard
- Tbsp mayonnaise
- Splash olive oil
- Seasoning
- Shake or two of celery salt
- Fennel fronds, finely chopped
- 2 tbsp flat-leaf parsley, roughly scissored

Toss the salad ingredients together in a large bowl and mix thoroughly. To serve, combine the crème fraîche with the vinegar, mustard, mayonnaise and olive oil and season generously. Stir in the celery salt and herbs then pour over the salad and stir in well. Decorate with the fennel fronds, roughly scissored.

MELON, TOMATO AND MINT

Simply a pleasant melange of zingy, fresh flavours. I like to use a couple of different melon varieties.

- 350g / 10 oz mixed melon chunks
- 2 large tomatoes, skinned and chopped (page 228)
- 150g / 6 oz cherry tomatoes including some yellow ones
- Handful fresh mint leaves, finely chopped
- Seasoning
- Vinaigrette (page 211)

Toss all in a bowl and serve.

CUCUMBER, OLIVE AND FLAT-LEAF PARSLEY

The perfect partner for red meats, poultry and fish.

- Cucumber, peeled and halved
- 100g / 4 oz green olives, pitted and halved
- 2 tbsp flat-leaf parsley, chopped
- Juice of ½ lemon
- Olive oil
- Seasoning

Slice both halves of the cucumber lengthways and seed. Cut into crescents and put in a bowl together with the olives and parsley. Dress with the lemon juice and oil and season plentifully.

WATERMELON, PARMA HAM, PUMPKIN SEED AND FETA

Cool and refreshing, this is one of my favourite summer salads. I often buy packets of ready sliced watermelon which are ideal for this purpose.

- 2 handfuls rocket, lamb's lettuce or pea shoot leaves, washed and picked over
- 4 generous watermelon wedges peeled, seeded and cut into bite-size chunks
- 4 - 5 slices Parma ham
- 150g / 6 oz feta
- 3 tbsp pumpkin seeds, dry toasted
- Flat-leaf parsley, roughly chopped

This looks splendid on a large white platter. Cover its base with the leaves then dot on the watermelon. Halve each slice of Parma ham and loosely fold then blob on plus the feta cheese. Scatter on the pumpkin seeds and flat-leaf parsley. I usually just dress with Vinaigrette (page 211).

Tips FROM THE SINK

- To primp up, replace parsley with finely chopped mint or a mixture of both.

Salads

Starters

The opening act of any lunch or dinner sets the tone for what follows. So, the essence and purpose of any starter is that they must invite, delight and titillate the senses, the eye and the palate simultaneously. Err on the side of smaller servings rather than over-facing guests with huge helpings.

SKAGEN PRAWNS
(SERVES 6)

This could be likened to a Swedish version of our own Prawn Cocktail but, instead of being mixed with shredded lettuce, it is best served on toasted sourdough or brioche. The spring onions and gherkins give it a nice bite to lift one's mood with their freshness and vigour.

- 500g / 1 lb good-quality cooked, peeled prawns
- Small bunch spring onions, white part only, into fine discs
- 6 gherkins, drained and finely diced
- ½ cucumber, peeled, seeded and finely chopped
- 2 tbsp fresh dill leaves, finely chopped
- 3 tbsp olive oil
- Juice and zest of ½ lemon
- 300ml / ½ pint sour cream
- Sea salt and freshly ground pepper
- Toasted sourdough or brioche bread
- Jar keta (salmon roe) - optional

Mix the prawns, spring onions, gherkins, cucumber and dill together in a large bowl. Combine the oil, lemon and sour cream in a jug, season and pour over the prawn mixture. Pile onto the pieces of toast and, if wished, decorate with a teaspoon or two of keta.

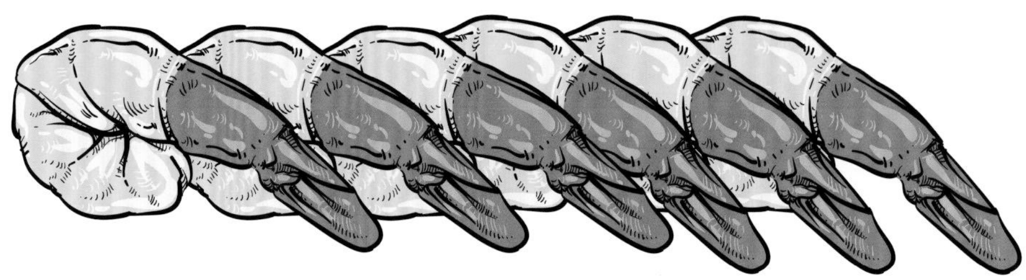

POTTED SHRIMPS
(SERVES 6)

As the cry goes, nothing beats a potted shrimp. Men fall upon these – they are viewed as the ultimate 'Club' food - perhaps these chaps were reared on them or possibly it's because they possess a nursery-like, nannying reassurance about them. I make kilo upon kilo of these every year at Christmas for clients and, although I will admit to being biased, I do think they are far nicer than the commercial brands whose layer of cake-like 'set' butter always reminds me of pots of Grip Fix glue.

- 250g / 8 oz peeled brown shrimps
- 180g / 6 oz butter, clarified (page 229)
- Bay leaf
- Cayenne pepper, to taste
- Pinch of mace
- Rasping of freshly grated nutmeg
- Juice of ½ lemon
- Tbsp anchovy essence
- Tbsp tarragon leaves, finely chopped
- White pepper and salt

Melt the butter in a saucepan together with the bay leaf, cayenne pepper, mace, nutmeg, lemon juice and anchovy essence and allow to bubble gently, but do not let it catch or brown. Remove from the heat and leave to infuse for 15 minutes before adding the shrimps. Take out the bay leaf then mix in the tarragon and season to taste. Divide the shrimps equally between six small pots or ramekins covering each with some butter then refrigerate. Serve room temperature with Fairy Toast (page 222) and lemon wedges.

Tips FROM THE SINK

- Try putting a teaspoon of potted shrimps (brought to room temperature) into a croustade for a really delicious canapé.

PARMESAN CUSTARDS WITH ANCHOVY TOAST (SERVES 6)

Rowley Leigh, one of the founder fathers of modern British cooking, used to have this on the menu when he cooked at Le Café Anglais. I (tentatively) wrote asking if he might share his secret. Being the generous chef he is, I was delighted when I received a printed card telling me how to make this little pot of ambrosial heaven. Clearly I wasn't the first person who had asked. It makes a marvellous savoury.

Custard:

- 300ml / ½ pint single cream
- 300ml / ½ pint milk
- 100g / 4 oz finely grated Parmesan
- 4 egg yolks
- Salt, ground white pepper and cayenne

Anchovy toast:

- 12 anchovy fillets
- 50g / 2 oz unsalted butter
- 8 slices pain de campagne or medium sliced white bread, crusts removed

Preheat the oven to 150 C. Mix the cream, milk and all bar one tablespoon of the cheese in a bowl and warm gently in a bowl over a pan of boiling water until the cheese has melted. Allow to cool completely before whisking in the egg yolks, salt, freshly milled pepper and a little cayenne pepper. Lightly butter 6 ramekins, or moulds of a similar size, and pour in the mixture. Place in a bain-marie and bake in the over for 15 minutes or so until just set.

To make the toast, mash the anchovies and butter to a smooth paste and spread over four of the slices of bread. Cover with the remaining slices and either toast in a sandwich maker or fry in oil until golden brown all over. Sprinkle the remaining Parmesan over the warm custards and brown under a hot grill. Cut the anchovy sandwiches into fingers and serve alongside.

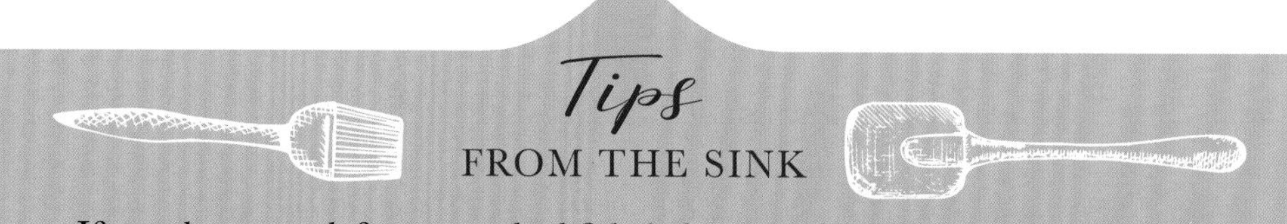

Tips FROM THE SINK

- If you have any leftover smoked fish (salmon or haddock), add this in flakes into the custards before baking.

Starters

SNAFFLES MOUSSE
(SERVES 6)

An old '70s cult favourite of the dinner party table. Snaffles was a fashionable basement restaurant in Dublin and this mousse was the signature dish of its proprietor Nick Tinne.

- Tin consommé - either chicken or beef
- 4 gelatine leaves
- 400g / 14 oz cream cheese (2 tubs)
- Heaped tsp curry powder
- Juice of ½ lemon
- Freshly ground white pepper
- 250g / 8 oz shelled prawns

Soak the gelatine leaves in a bowl of cold water until soft and spongy then remove and squeeze out excess liquid. Heat a little of the consommé in a saucepan and add the gelatine, heating gently until it has dissolved then bung into the food processor together with the rest of the consommé, cream cheese, curry power, lemon juice and pepper. Whizz until smooth then pour into ramekins, cover and put in the fridge to set. Decorate with the prawns and serve with Fairy Toast (page 222).

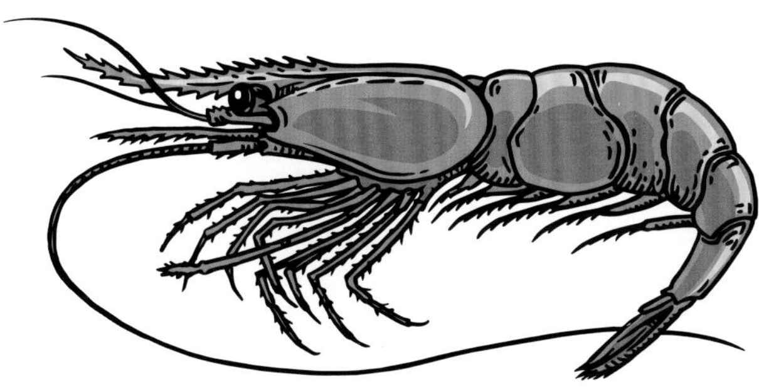

PEA MOUSSES
(SERVES 6)

These are a delicate green, look elegant and can be prepped well ahead.

- Large shallot or small onion, peeled and finely chopped
- 50g / 2 oz butter
- 400g / 14 oz frozen peas - I use the ordinary, garden variety
- 300ml / ½ pint double cream
- 3 eggs
- Tbsp tarragon leaves, very finely chopped
- Seasoning

Preheat the oven to 170. Heat the butter in a pan and sweat the shallot/onion until soft but not coloured. Add the peas and 2 tbsp water and cook for 3 - 4 minutes. Scrape the mixture into a food processor and add the cream and blend until smooth. Next, add the eggs and whizz again then season to taste. Pass through a sieve and stir in the tarragon leaves. Line ramekins or individual moulds with cling film (dampen the insides to get the cling to stick) if you intend turning the mousses out to serve - if not, don't bother. Pour the mixture into them and place the ramekins in a roasting tray sitting on a baking sheet for ease of handling. Pour boiling water into the tray to ⅔ of the way up the sides of the ramekins. Cover loosely with a sheet of greaseproof paper and cook in the oven for approximately 25 - 30 minutes until the tops are firm. Remove from the oven and lift the ramekins out of their water bath then, when cool enough to handle, turn out onto individual plates if you wish.

Serve with pea shoots and perhaps a small salad with bacon lardons. For real elegance, hand round Parmesan Crisps (page 170).

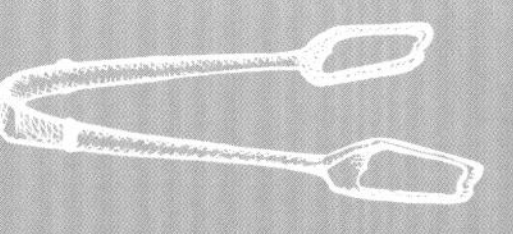

Tips
FROM THE SINK

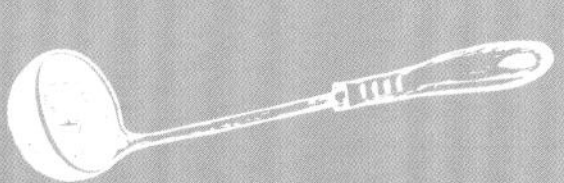

- To fancy this dish up, simply melt down a tub or two of Potted Shrimps (page 39) in a saucepan until the butter is liquid, add a dash of double cream and a splash of white wine then pour this sauce around the mousses.

SMOKED SALMON AND PRAWN MOUSSE (SERVES 6 - 8)

Unfailingly redolent of the 'Prawn Cocktail' era, but nonetheless it is a good stalwart and never disappoints.

- 250g / 8 oz packet of smoked salmon trimmings – available at supermarkets
- 200g / 6 oz shelled fresh prawns, blotted on kitchen paper to remove excess water
- 600ml / 1 pint crème fraîche
- Large tbsp dill or tarragon and basil leaves, chopped or finely scissored
- 4 gelatine leaves
- ¼ glass white wine or Noilly Prat
- Juice of a lemon
- 2 - 3 egg whites (keep the yolks for making mayonnaise)
- Seasoning

Soak the leaves of gelatine in a bowl of cold water and leave for at least 10 minutes until soft and spongy. Meanwhile, put the salmon pieces in a food processor and whizz together to chop up further then add the crème fraîche and blend again. Add the herbs, lemon juice and seasoning. When the gelatine is soft, lift the leaves out of the bowl and gently but firmly squeeze out all the liquid. Put all into a small saucepan and melt over a gentle heat together with the wine or Noilly Prat. When gelatine has dissolved, whizz into the salmon mixture. In a separate bowl, whisk the egg whites until completely stiff then, using a metal spoon, fold in the salmon and finally stir in the prawns. Transfer the mixture either into a ring mould which has been filled with cold water and this then emptied out (this helps when it comes to turning out the mousse) or into a large soufflé dish or 8 individual ramekins. Leave in the fridge for at least 3 hours to set.

To serve, if in a mould, dip the base of this into a basin of hand hot water then invert onto a large flat plate and shake to turn out – you'll hear the mousse 'plop'.

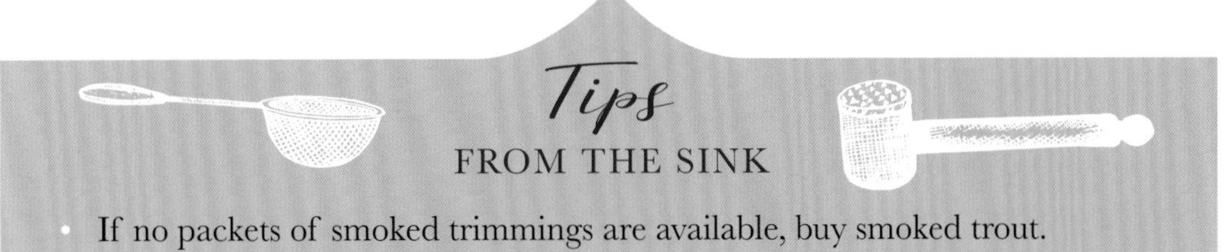

Tips
FROM THE SINK

- If no packets of smoked trimmings are available, buy smoked trout.

Starters

GARLIC PRAWNS WITH GUACAMOLE

Guacamole:

- 2 - 3 ripe avocados
- Juice of 1 - 2 limes
- 2 firm, ripe tomatoes, skinned (page 228), seeded and cored then finely diced - optional
- Small red chilli, seeded and finely chopped
- Sea salt
- Glug of olive oil

Optional extras:

Depending upon how much 'zip' you want in your guacamole, listed below are some other ingredients guaranteed to 'pep' it up.

- Tbsp coriander leaves, finely chopped
- Crushed garlic – to taste
- Paprika/cayenne pepper

Halve, stone and peel the avocados then mash on a plate with a fork until they are pretty much smooth – the odd lump is fine and adds a bit of texture. Next, stir in the lime juice, chilli, tomato flesh, sea salt and olive oil. Plop the avocado stone into the mixture, cover tightly with cling film to prevent discolouring until ready to use at which point remove the stone.

Prawns:

- 375g / 12 oz shelled raw prawns
- 1 - 2 garlic cloves, peeled and crushed
- 2 tbsp olive oil
- 50g / 2 oz butter
- Squeeze lemon or lime juice

For the prawns, put these in a bowl together with the garlic and oil and leave covered, in a cool place, for anything between 10 minutes and 24 hours. To cook, heat a knob of butter in a non-stick frying pan then add the garlic. When sizzling - but not burning - chuck in the prawns, together with the oil, and move around the pan. They will quickly turn pink so flip them over and sauté until cooked. Spritz with a squirt of either lemon or lime juice then remove from the heat. Dish up the prawns, pour on the juices and serve alongside the guacamole.

TUNA TARTARE

All too often, receipts for 'raw' fish seem to involve a host of overpowering ingredients - endless doses of wasabi paste, ginger, spring onions, soy and other cloying sauces merely mask its natural flavour so, use other adjuncts judiciously. Choose only the finest quality yellowfin tuna which should be deep red, almost maroony brown, with a pleasing plumpness about it and very firm to the touch. If you cannot find the perfect tuna then change your menu. That old adage about making a silk purse out of a sow's ear has never held truer than where this particular fish and dish is concerned.

- 500g / 1 lb best quality loin of tuna, middle cut
- Olive oil
- Tbsp scissored chives, plus extra for garnish
- Zest of a small lemon
- Squirt or two of lemon juice
- Shake of toasted sesame oil
- ½ tsp runny honey
- Freshly milled salt and white peppercorns
- 50g / 2 oz hazelnuts, toasted and sliced

Wrap the tuna tightly in cling film and place in the freezer for 15 minutes or so to make slicing it easier. Meanwhile, mix together all the other ingredients – bar the hazelnuts – in a bowl.

To serve, remove the tuna from the freezer, place on a board and, using a very sharp knife, slice as thinly as you can. Arrange on a plate and spoon over the dressing. Finish by scattering over the bits of toasted hazelnuts and a few more chives.

BEETROOT-CURED SALMON WITH DILL CRÈME FRAÎCHE

(SERVES 10 – 12)

This colourful dish is an absolute show-stopper. Plain old gravadlax is unlikely ever to get so much as a look-in again as far as I am concerned. I can guarantee that the effort involved pays dividends when you bring this stunning dish to the table. In case you feel it is rather hard work, take comfort in the fact it is best made a week in advance and it also freezes beautifully.

- Whole side of salmon, scaled and filleted, skin on
- 2 tbsp coriander seeds
- 2 tbsp fennel seeds
- Tbsp black peppercorns
- 3 tbsp sea salt
- 3 tbsp granulated sugar
- 3 tbsp vodka
- Grated zest of one lemon
- Grated zest of one orange
- Bunch raw beetroot, peeled and grated
- Bunch fresh dill, chopped

Dill Sauce:

- Bunch dill leaves, chopped
- Salt & freshly ground black pepper
- 300g / ½ pint crème fraîche
- 2 tsp Dijon mustard
- Tbsp red wine vinegar
- Splash of milk

Remove any pin bones from the fillet with tweezers or, better still, smile sweetly at your fishmonger and get him to do this bit for you! Next, line a baking tray with cling film (allowing plenty of overlap) and put the fish on it, skin side down. Grind the coriander and fennel seeds with the peppercorns but make sure they retain a bit of texture and are not just powder. Combine with the salt, sugar, vodka, lemon and orange zest and the beetroot and then mix in the dill. Spread the mixture all over the surface of the fish and press down then wrap tightly in the cling film. Place another baking tray on top and weight down with weights, jars or tins. Leave in the fridge for anything up to 6 days, periodically unwrapping and spooning the liquid back over (similar to basting), then re-cover and weight again.

For the dill sauce, mix the crème fraîche, mustard and vinegar together and season well then stir in the dill and add enough milk for a sloppy consistency.

To serve – starting at the tail end – and with a very sharp knife, cut very thin slices from the fish at a 45-degree angle and arrange on individual plates splashed with a little dressing.

- Any remaining bits of the salmon can be mixed together with red chicory leaves, blood oranges (when in season otherwise use ordinary), toasted walnuts and chunks of avocado. Pour the juices into some vinaigrette and shake well to use as the dressing. Decorate with flat-leaf parsley roughly scissored. This is a picture on a plate!!

FRED'S BLOODY OYSTERS

The description 'Bon Viveur' could have been invented for Fred Carr. His own appearance and approach to food leave no one in any doubt that here is someone who loves good cuisine. His appreciation is equalled by his understanding and passion for proper, well-sourced ingredients and he is one of the best natural cooks I know. He arrived for lunch one sunny day bearing a large tray. Sitting on a bed of crushed ice were these oysters in their own jellied Bloody Mary. I felt sorry for the other guests who had come bearing boxes of chocolates and pots of marmalade. This platter shrieks of style and, on that day, firmly put my own meagre canapés into the shade.

- 24 rock oysters
- Tbsp flat-leaf parsley leaves, chopped
- 4 leaf gelatine sheets, soaked in a bowl of cold water
- Lemon quarters, to serve

Bloody Mary:

- Vodka
- 200ml / just under ½ pint Clamato juice
- Lemon juice
- Worcester sauce
- Tabasco, to taste

Open the oysters, (page 227) sieving the juices into a jug and put the molluscs and their shells to one side. Add the Bloody Mary mixture ingredients to the oyster juices. When the gelatine leaves are completely soft and spongy squeeze out the excess liquid and warm through very gently to melt. Stir into the Bloody Mary mix together with the flat-leaf parsley. Spread crushed ice over the base of a large, flat platter then wedge the oyster shells into the ice so that they don't wobble. Spoon a little sauce into each shell, add an oyster and pour over a little more sauce. Refrigerate to set. If necessary, top up with more Bloody Mary. Serve straight from the fridge with lemon quarters.

CHICKEN LIVER PARFAIT

There are any number of receipts for this dish and I think this one ticks all the boxes. It's quick and easy to make and tastes excellent. Serve with Fairy Toast (page 222) and My Ma's Chutney (page 201) or, just as good, Cranberry, Plum and Star Anise Compote (page 204)

- 200g / 7 oz butter
- Shallot, peeled and finely diced
- Bay leaf
- 2 plump garlic cloves, peeled and finely chopped
- Pinch freshly grated nutmeg
- Pinch ground allspice
- 500g / 1 lb chicken livers, trimmed of any sinew and drained
- Generous slug each of brandy and Madeira
- 3 tbsp double cream / crème fraîche
- Seasoning

Melt 50g / 2 oz of the butter in a large saucepan and gently sauté the shallot with the bay leaf until soft and translucent. Add the garlic and spices and then the chicken livers. Cook over a high heat for 3 – 4 minutes until lightly browned. They should be pinkish inside so cut through one to check. Pour in the alcohol and boil hard briefly or until most of the liquid has evaporated. Transfer to the food processor and season well. Melt the remainder of the butter in the pan and, as you blend the chicken liver mixture, pour in the butter. Taste and finally add the cream or crème fraîche and whizz to combine. Sieve the mixture (this may sound a fag but it only takes a couple of minutes and is well worth the effort). Pour into individual ramekins or one large dish. This keeps well for up to one week in the fridge.

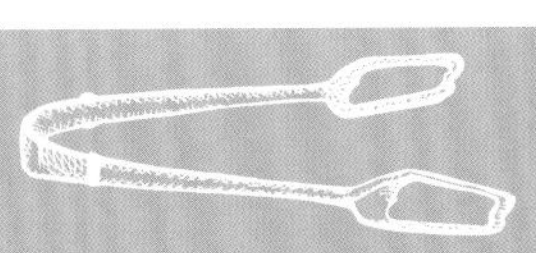

Tips FROM THE SINK

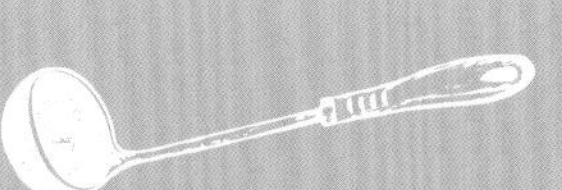

- Best made a couple of days before eaten which allows its flavours to develop.

Starters

TWICE-BAKED CRAB SOUFFLÉS

I used to scoff at these soufflés protesting they are twice the work. Well, that was then – but now I am a convert. Yes, they're rich on account of the fact the second time they are cooked it's in a cream bath, but they're a fabulous, fail-safe dish to trot out. Their greatest joy is that they can all be prepped ahead. They also freeze very happily and can be cooked straight from frozen.

- 425 ml / ¾ pint milk
- Rasping of nutmeg
- 75g / 3 oz butter
- 75g / 3 oz plain flour
- Shallot, peeled and studded with cloves
- 200g / 6 oz Emmental, grated plus extra for finishing off
- 350g / 12 oz white crab meat
- Tbsp English mustard
- 6 eggs, separated
- Tbsp chives, scissored
- 500g / 1 lb spinach, blanched
- 300ml / ½ pint double cream

Preheat the oven to 190 C. Butter 8 ordinary sized ramekins or 4 large ones and place in the fridge to chill. Heat the milk with the nutmeg. Make a roux with the butter and flour, then add the milk and stir well until smooth. Mix in the cheese, egg yolks, mustard, crab and chives and season. In a large clean bowl, whisk the egg whites and fold into the cheese sauce. Divide the mixture between the ramekins and stand these in a roasting tin and fill with boiling water. Cook for 25 minutes just until nicely risen. Remove and leave to cool. At this stage the soufflés may, if wished, be individually wrapped and frozen. If using immediately, turn out into a large buttered ovenproof dish, in which are arranged the appropriate number of spinach 'blobs'. Pour over the cream, sprinkle the surfaces with the remaining cheese and bake in the oven at 190 C for 8 - 10 minutes, then serve.

ICED PEPPER POTS WITH PESTO

(SERVES 6)

If you wish, cheat with this one by using a jar of ready - roasted peppers which will then involve zero cooking. It's ideal for balmy (!) summer days and is also chic enough to serve for dinner parties.

- 2 - 3 large roasted red peppers (page 228) or jar ready-roasted peppers, roughly chopped
- Paprika
- Crème fraîche
- Pesto – fresh ready-made is fine

Preheat the oven to 190 C. Place peppers in a food processor and whizz until smooth. Season with the paprika, according to how spicy you like these things, then blend in a blob or two of crème fraîche. Push through a sieve and that's it - FINITO! Spoon into small little pots, ramekins or even old teacups and add a teaspoon of pesto to the top. Chill before serving alongside Fairy Toast (page 222).

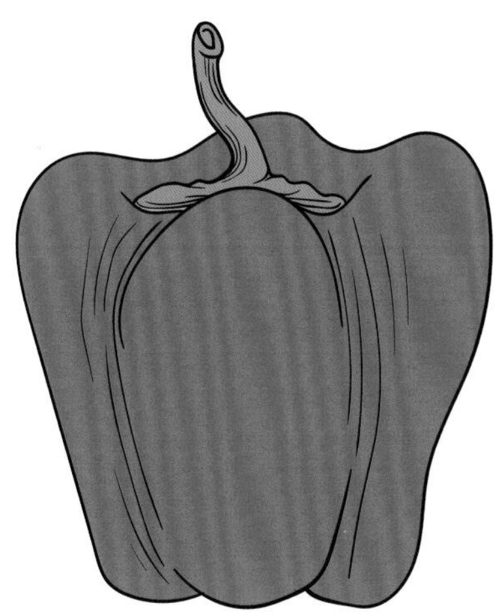

Starters

TOAST-RACK TOMATOES

The ultimate easy-peasy, no-cook little number. It's a masterpiece in three ingredients and, providing the tomatoes are not insipid, it transports one instantly to images of Mediterranean summer days.

- 4 large ripe, flavoursome tomatoes
- 2 buffalo mozzarella
- Fresh basil leaves
- Olive oil
- Seasoning

Remove the stalks from each tomato and sit, calyx end (bums) down, on 4 plates. Using a serrated knife, slice each tomato almost, but not quite, through to the base, rather as though preparing a stick of French bread in readiness to receive garlic butter.

Fan open gently and sprinkle with sea salt, black pepper and dot a few torn basil leaves between each slice. Slice the mozzarella to size with a sharp knife and insert them into the tomatoes, like white pieces of 'toast'. Drizzle with the olive oil between each slice as you go.

Pour a little more oil over the top and scatter with more basil before serving alongside warmed ciabatta bread to mop up the juices.

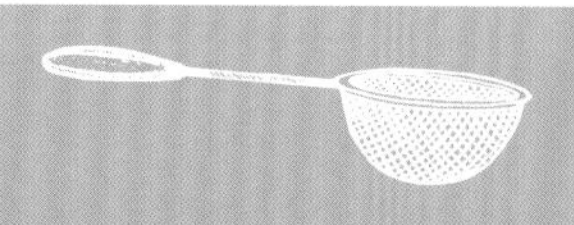

Tips FROM THE SINK

- Sniff the tomatoes before buying. If they exude a good, ripe smell then you are already halfway towards producing a delicious dish. If, on the other hand, they don't, then give up and change the menu.
- Fresh pesto (available in most supermarkets) would also be good drizzled over these tomatoes.

TURKISH-BAKED AUBERGINES WITH CHILLI, FETA AND MINT

This is my own simpler interpretation of Imam Bayildi and a great deal swifter to prepare. I love the combo of textures and temperatures. It is best served at room temperature.

- 4 aubergines
- Olive oil
- Seasoning
- 2 onions, peeled and finely sliced
- 2 garlic cloves, peeled and crushed
- 2 small red chillies, halved, seeded and finely diced
- Juice of ½ lemon
- 100g / 4 oz feta, crumbled
- 200g / 7oz Greek yoghurt
- Handful of mint leaves, torn
- Olive oil, to drizzle

Preheat the oven to 200 C. Halve the aubergines lengthways and score a trellis pattern into the flesh of each half on the cut surface and arrange in a dish. Steep them in olive oil and season generously, turning them over to ensure they are well coated then place them in the oven and roast for 40 - 45 minutes.

Whilst the aubergines are cooking, sauté the onions in one tbsp olive oil until soft and golden but not burnt. Add the garlic and chilli and cook for a further 2 minutes until they are soft. Once the aubergines are tender, put them on a serving platter or dish, cut side up and squeeze the lemon juice over them. Gently press the cooked flesh down to make some room for the onions and fill the aubergine cavities with the onion and chilli mix and scatter the feta on top. Dab blobs of the yoghurt over the aubergines and throw over the mint leaves. Drizzle with olive oil before serving either warm or at room temperature but, whichever way, with lots of warmed crusty bread.

- Hand round with a bowl of yoghurt with more chopped mint and a few dashes of Tabasco to add a little pep.

Rice, Pasta & More

Apart from the obvious beauty of Italy, it is also famously known as the home of pasta as well as a great many rice dishes - all of which have originated from specific regions throughout the country. Each one possesses a history and majesty of its own. The Italians serve these two simplest of ingredients with such aplomb yet total lack of pretension that one often wonders why anyone ever considers eating anything else. As Brits, we've come a long way from the days of 'spag bol' - good though it is when properly cooked - and every larder and store cupboard should be stocked with several varieties of dried rice and pasta which, with a little imagination, can be transformed into a never-ending range of delicious receipts, satisfying without being either over-rich on the palate or expensive on the pocket. Here are some to tempt you.

VINCISGRASSI
(SERVES 6 - 8)

This Italian dish is a speciality of the Marche region where they make one version with meat and the other, as shown here, simply with some Parma ham.

Mushroom Sauce:

- 450g / 12 oz mixed fresh mushrooms, sliced
- 25g / 1 oz dried mushrooms i.e. porcini, soaked in boiling water
- 25g / 1 oz butter
- Olive oil
- Seasoning
- 200g / 7 oz Parma ham, cut into narrow strips

Béchamel:

- 1.2 litres / 2 pints milk
- ½ onion
- 2 bay leaves
- Peppercorns
- 50g / 2 oz butter
- 75g / 3 oz plain flour
- Tbsp flat-leaf parsley, chopped
- 175ml / ¼ pint double cream

- 500g / 1 lb packet ready-cooked pasta sheets
- 50g / 2 oz Parmesan, grated
- Truffle oil, to taste

Fry off dried mushrooms and mix with the Parma ham. Melt butter and ½ tbsp olive oil and sauté mushrooms in batches, seasoning.

For the béchamel, heat milk with onion, bay leaves, and peppercorns, then remove from the heat to infuse for 30 minutes. Melt butter in a pan, make a roux by adding the flour and cook for 2 minutes before pouring in the strained milk mixture, whisking until smooth. Add cream, fungi, ham and parsley then season well.

To assemble, layer the cooked pasta sheets, followed by the sauce, grated cheese and repeat finishing with sauce and cheese. Bake for 20 minutes and drizzle with truffle oil before serving.

SPINACH, PEA AND BACON RISOTTO

I find all that continuous stirring, good for the mind, body and soul. The rice you use will have an impact - Arborio is the most widely available though many Italians favour Carnaroli as they believe it makes the creamiest risotto, whilst Vialone produces a more soupy, flowing risotto. Remember, a risotto stands or falls by the goodness of the stock you use, and this needs to be added hot so keep the pot simmering constantly.

- 2 shallots, finely chopped
- Olive oil
- 75g / 3 oz butter
- Garlic clove, peeled and crushed
- 300g / 10 oz risotto rice, Arborio or Carnaroli
- Glass white wine
- 1 ¼ litres / 2 pints 4 fl oz chicken or vegetable stock, hot
- 250g / 8 oz peas, cooked and kept warm
- 1kg / 2.2 lbs spinach leaves, cooked, drained and puréed, kept warm
- 100g / 4 oz bacon, cooked and cut into pieces
- Seasoning
- 100g / 4 oz Parmesan, grated

Heat the oil and half the butter in a heavy frying pan and cook the shallots over a medium heat until soft but not coloured, adding the garlic halfway through. Add the rice and stir it well into the fat and juices until it is translucent. Pour in the wine and mix well and once this has disappeared, start adding the stock a ladle at a time. It is important not to add any further liquid until the previous ladleful has been absorbed. Never drown the rice in liquid. Stir constantly as this gives it the best consistency. When it is perfectly cooked (as a rough guide, cooking time is usually around 20 minutes from the first addition of stock, with just a hint of a bite in the centre of the grain) add the vegetables and bacon. Throw in the remaining butter and half the cheese and stir gently. Don't add the Parmesan before the end otherwise the cheese makes the risotto too sticky and gluey. Cover and leave to stand for two minutes then serve with the rest of the Parmesan.

KEDGEREE

An Anglo-Indian concoction, this is a king amongst breakfast dishes, and is also perfect for brunch, lunch, suppers or midnight snacks. This is a 'straight-up' version though it can also be made by cooking the rice in coconut milk with crushed cardamon seeds and garnished with coriander.

- 750g / 1 ½ lbs undyed smoked haddock
- Bay leaf
- 75g / 3 oz butter
- Onion, peeled and finely chopped
- Heaped tsp curry powder
- Long-grain white rice, measured up to 225 ml / 8 fl oz level in a jug
- Haddock cooking liquid, measured to 450 ml / 16 fl oz level in a jug
- 3 hard-boiled eggs, each half cut into thirds
- 250g / 8 oz shelled cooked prawns
- 3 tbsp flat-leaf parsley, chopped
- Juice of ½ lemon
- Grated nutmeg
- Freshly ground black pepper

Preheat the oven to 180 C. Place the haddock fillets in an ovenproof dish and cover with 600ml / 1 pint cold water. Add the bay leaf, cover with tin foil and cook in the oven until the fish is just done, about 10 - 12 minutes. Remove the fish, transfer to a dish, cover and keep warm. Drain the cooking liquid into a measuring jug.

Next, melt 50g / 2 oz of the butter in a saucepan and soften the onion for approximately 5 minutes then stir in the curry powder followed by the measured rice and mix well. Pour in 450ml / 16 fl oz of the haddock cooking water and stir. When it comes to simmering point, cover with a tightly fitting lid and cook, very gently, for 15 minutes until the rice is tender. Meanwhile, remove the skin from the fish and break it into flakes, discarding any bones. Once the rice is done, remove from the heat, fluff it up with a fork before adding the haddock, eggs, prawns, parsley, lemon juice, nutmeg, pepper and the last bit of butter. Cover the pan with a clean folded tea towel and leave it on a very gentle heat for a few minutes then pile onto a warmed serving dish. Serve with Tomato Salsa (page 218) or Wild Garlic Pesto (page 214).

WILD RICE & BLUE CHEESE SALAD
(SERVES 6 - 8)

This sings of summer and is excellent for entertaining as part of a buffet as well as for picnics.

- 250g / 8 oz basmati and wild rice
- 6 sun-dried tomatoes, chopped into small pieces
- 3 tbsp small capers, drained
- Zest of a lemon
- 100g / 4 oz pine nuts
- 2 courgettes, grated
- 50g / 2 oz mild blue cheese, crumbled
- Flat-leaf parsley leaves, finely chopped
- Seasoning

Cook the rice in boiling salted water for 25 - 30 minutes until fairly soft. Drain under running cold water and set aside in the sieve to get rid of any excess liquid.

Turn into a large bowl and add all the other ingredients. Check seasoning. I usually stir in a few tablespoons of vinaigrette and mix in thoroughly.

SPAGHETTI CARBONARA
(SERVES 2)

This is my 'go-to' supper dish when I am running late and have failed to go shopping. It takes minutes to make and I love its utter simplicity and homeliness.

- 3 egg yolks
- 50g / 2 oz Parmesan, finely grated
- Seasoning
- 5 - 6 rashers streaky bacon, thinly sliced or 150g / 6 oz pancetta, skin removed
- 200g / 7 oz dried spaghetti
- Olive oil

Put the egg yolks into a bowl, add the Parmesan, season well and mix with a fork and set to one side.

Next, using a frying pan, cook the bacon or, if using pancetta, chop into small pieces and cook for 3 - 4 minutes or until it starts to crisp up.

Cook the spaghetti in a pan of boiling, salted water with a splash of olive oil until 'al dente' then drain, reserving some of the cooking liquid. Add the spaghetti to the frying pan and toss well over the heat then remove the pan from the stove. Add a splash of cooking water, leave everything for a couple of minutes to cool, then pour in the egg mixture and mix well. Add a little more cooking water until the spaghetti is shining.

Serve with a bowl of grated Parmesan and some black pepper.

Tips FROM THE SINK

- Any leftovers will heat up successfully providing this is done over a very gentle heat.

HARRY'S BAR TAGLIATELLE

Easy to cook and just as easy to eat.

- 3 tbsp butter
- 50g / 2 oz prosciutto, cut into strips
- 350g / 10 oz dried tagliatelle
- 50g / 2 oz Parmesan, grated plus extra for serving
- 500ml / $\frac{3}{4}$ - 1 pint béchamel sauce (page 212), warm
- Seasoning

Preheat the grill. Melt a nut of the butter in a large ovenproof frying pan and add the prosciutto. Cook for a minute or two stirring constantly. In a large pan of boiling, salted water (to which a slick of olive oil has been added) cook the pasta until 'al dente'. Drain and put into the frying pan plus the remaining butter and half the Parmesan. Toss well then spoon over the béchamel sauce. Sprinkle with the remaining Parmesan and place under the grill until hot and bubbling. Serve immediately with additional Parmesan straight from the pan.

LINGUINE WITH CRAB AND CHILLI

- 500g / 1 lb dressed crab (around 2 large crabs)
- 5 tbsp olive oil, plus extra for drizzling
- 2 garlic cloves, peeled and finely chopped
- Red chilli, seeded and finely diced
- 4 tbsp flat-leaf parsley, chopped
- Zest and juice of one lemon
- Seasoning
- 500g / 1 lb dried linguine

Mix the crab meats, white and brown, together. Heat the oil in a large frying pan and lightly fry the garlic and chilli for no more than a minute, releasing their flavours. Add the crab, parsley, lemon zest and juice until warmed through. Season and set aside. Cook the pasta until 'al dente' and drain, reserving a little of the cooking water to loosen if necessary. Add the pasta to the crab mixture in the frying pan then stir to combine everything over a gentle heat. Pour in a drizzle of olive oil plus a little cooking water to loosen. Check seasoning and serve immediately.

FOUR-CHEESE MACARONI
(SERVES 6)

Nursery food this may well be but it is still one of the world's supreme comfort dishes with its unctuously rich cheesy overtones. I use a combination of mozzarella, mascarpone, Parmesan and Gruyère cheeses - that way you can have a competition for the longest strings of melted cheese from pan to mouth.

- 250g / 8 oz macaroni pasta
- Olive oil
- 250g / 8 oz mascarpone
- 250ml / scant ½ pint whole milk
- 450ml / ¾ pint double cream
- 175g / 7 oz Parmesan, grated
- 250g / 8 oz mozzarella, grated (available in packets)
- 75g / 3 oz Gruyère, grated
- Heaped tsp Dijon mustard
- Seasoning
- Generous rasping of nutmeg
- 4 tbsp breadcrumbs

Bring a large pan of salted water to a rolling boil, add a slug of olive oil and then the pasta. When the water returns to the boil, turn it down to a medium heat and simmer for approx 10 - 12 minutes until done then drain. In the meantime, using a spoon or fork, beat the mascarpone to soften in a large bowl then add the milk, cream, Parmesan, mozzarella, half the Gruyère, mustard, seasoning and nutmeg. Tip the hot pasta into this sauce and mix thoroughly then transfer to a large ovenproof baking dish or individual ones. Mix the remaining Parmesan with the breadcrumbs and sprinkle over. This may be prepared in advance to this stage.

To cook, preheat the oven to 200 C. Bake in the oven until golden brown and bubbling for 25 - 30 minutes for one large dish and 15 - 20 minutes for smaller ones.

PARMIGIANA
(SERVES 6 - 8)

This is one of my favourite no-nonsense Italian style dishes - yes, it is a bit of a fiddle to make but, once assembled, it only needs reheating and it is ready to bring to the table.

- 3 tbsp good olive oil
- 2 garlic cloves, peeled and finely chopped
- 2 x 680 ml / 2 x 1 pint jars of passata
- 2 tbsp torn basil leaves, plus a few extra for decoration
- 75g / 3 oz Parmesan, plus a little extra to serve, grated
- Sunflower oil, for frying
- 1 kg / 2.3 lbs aubergines, ends removed, and thinly sliced
- 3 courgettes, ends removed, sliced
- 2 mozzarella, drained and sliced

Preheat the oven to 200 C. Begin by making the sauce by heating the olive oil in a saucepan. Add the garlic and fry briefly until fragrant - don't allow it to 'catch'. Next, add the passata plus half of one of the jars filled with water, the torn basil and a little salt. Bring to the boil and simmer over a medium-low heat for about 40 minutes until you have a thick pouring sauce. Heat the sunflower oil in a frying pan and cook the aubergine slices in batches frying until crispy and a light golden colour on each side then drain on kitchen paper. Do the same with the courgettes adding more oil if necessary.

To assemble, line the base of a 35 x 25 cm / 14 x 10" baking dish with a thin layer of sauce, arrange a layer of aubergines and courgettes lengthways on top so that they overlap slightly, then add another layer of sauce, a couple of tablespoons of the grated Parmesan and half the mozzarella. Repeat, this time layering the vegetables crossways, spoon over the sauce and then add the final layer of aubergines and courgettes, again lengthways. Finish off with a layer of tomato sauce so that the vegetables are liberally covered and sprinkle over the Parmesan and cover with foil.

Bake in the oven for 45 minutes, then remove the foil and bake for a further 25 - 30 minutes until lightly golden. Leave to stand for 15 minutes then serve either hot or at room temperature with a little more Parmesan and decorated with the remaining basil leaves.

Tips FROM THE SINK

- If you have some tomato sauce left over, use it to serve with pasta.

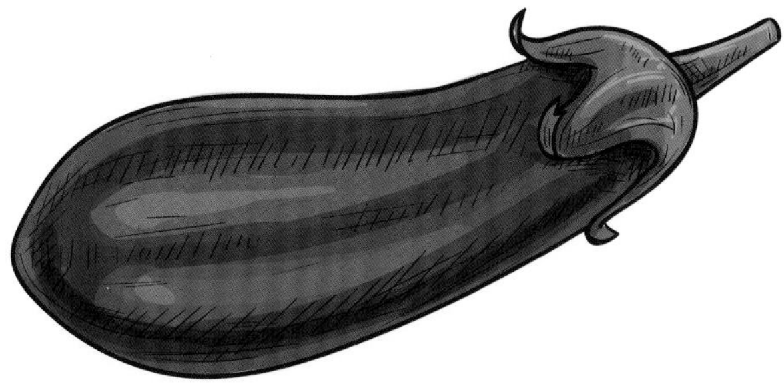

FORATA DI SPINACI
(SERVES 6)

This dish comes from my good friend John Penrose so I will let him tell you about it in his own words.

This Italian dish is more correctly known as sformato di spinaci, *a flan or tart that bears absolutely no resemblance to Popeye's can of greens. Packed with eggs, heavy cream and Parmesan, it is anything but a body building fitness food.*

The word sformato *in Italian means deformed or misshapen. The dish is simple, yet versatile, hailing from the Abruzzi region and is a firm favourite amongst all who know it - being demanded and devoured from the hill towns of Umbria and Tuscany, to the Gloucestershire Cotswolds and even as far as the Minnesota wilderness.*

Sformato *is a curious description because many recipes call for it to be formed in a mould or dish before baking but here's how it's made:*

- 1 ½ kg / 3 lbs spinach, blanched
- 3 eggs
- 600 ml / 1 pint double cream
- 250g / 8 oz Parmesan, grated
- Couple pinches freshly grated nutmeg
- Seasoning

Preheat the oven to 180 C. Combine the eggs, cream, then the nutmeg, salt and pepper in a large bowl.

Blanch the spinach – it can be fresh from the garden or market stall, washed and drained, or ready-washed supermarket spinach, even frozen, but buy leaves, not chopped. Some recipes call for the tough stalks to be removed but I like my sformato with bit of a bite so do not lose them all. Ensure that every drop of water is squeezed from the spinach.

This is very important if you want to avoid ending up with a wishy-washy imitation of spinach soup. Chop coarsely and combine with the creamy mixture.

Add the freshly grated Parmesan. I also throw in some large lumps of shaved pieces of the cheese to give the tart a little body. Pour into a baking dish - the spinach mixture should be at least a couple of inches deep.

Bake uncovered for about 35 minutes. The top should be browned and slightly crusty, the spinach still creamy. Serve hot.

Fish

Nothing compares to fabulously fresh fish, simply cooked. The trick of course lies in selecting only the finest. When choosing, buy by eye and consult your trusty fishmonger. He will always know what is best on the day. Remember too that fish is seasonal.

I go to Severn & Wye Smokery near Gloucester, for my fish. Their counter has a magnificent array of species which I liken to being in a piscatorial candy store! Weather dependent, and at the correct time of the year for each type of fish, you will find mackerel, kippers, sardines, hake, halibut, turbot, tuna, salmon and sea trout, cod, haddock, scallops, mussels, crabs, lobsters, langoustine, sea bass, bream, Dover, lemon and slip soles - the list is endless. They will skin, fillet and scale for you as well as offering advice, suggestions and ideas as to how to cook whatever one decides upon. As their name suggests, Severn & Wye also have their own smokery and their produce is smoked over a blend of oak chips and chipped whisky and Calvados barrels. It is well worth a visit. Further north, on the Isle of Lewis, Uig Lodge also produce excellent smoked salmon products and every Christmas they send great polysterene boxes filled with sides of salmon, all beautifully hand-sliced for ***Dishes with Dashers*** clients.

FISH PARCELS

A novel way of presenting a 'fishy on a dishy'. It's a one-stop-receipt as that little package contains everything the diner could want: fish, vegetables and a jus/sauce and, of course, the aroma as each person opens up their own helping is mouth-wateringly good.

- Roll of strong aluminium foil
- 350g / 12 oz fish i.e. haddock, sea bass, salmon, raw prawns etc. - either a mixture or one type, skinned and boned where appropriate
- 3 - 4 new potatoes per person, cooked and neatly cubed
- 3 - 4 vine cherry tomatoes per person
- Lemon slices and juice of a lemon
- 2 lemongrass stalks, tough outer leaves removed and roughly chopped
- Handful of herbs such as parsley, tarragon, basil, rosemary or thyme
- Large glass of white wine
- 50g / 2 oz butter
- Seasoning

Preheat the oven to 200 C. Cut four very large squares of tin foil (approx 22cm / 10" square). Chop the fish into bite-sized pieces and place some on each sheet of foil. Add the potatoes and tomatoes followed by the lemon slices and juice, lemongrass, herbs and, bringing the four corners of each piece of foil upwards, pour the wine, equally divided, into each one. Dot with little flecks of butter and add some seasoning. Crimp the top of each package so it is sealed, then stand in a roasting tin and cook for approx 12 minutes. (To check whether it is ready simply undo the top and take a peek inside). If ready, the white fish will be opaque and prawns (and salmon if using) will have turned pink. Plonk individual packages into bowls and place in front of each person, leaving them to unwrap their own dinner and savour their delicious fragrance.

Tips
FROM THE SINK

- Try adding some quickly blanched sugar snap peas or raw spinach leaves to the parcels for a bit of greenery.

Fish

Fish

SALMON TERIYAKI WITH WILTED GREENS

Mirin - Japanese rice wine - adds to the piquancy of this sweetly lacquered fish.

- 3 tbsp sake (or very dry sherry)
- Tsp caster sugar
- 3 tbsp soy sauce
- 3 tbsp mirin
- 2 tbsp root ginger, peeled and grated
- 4 x 150g / 6 oz salmon fillets, middle cut, skin on
- Groundnut or vegetable oil
- Juice of a lime
- Bunch spring onions, trimmed and cut into slices at an angle
- 2 garlic cloves, peeled and very finely chopped
- 4 pak choi

Whisk the sake (or alternative), sugar, soy, mirin and ginger together and pour over the fish then leave to marinate for up to 3 hours. Drain the marinade into a pan and boil for a few minutes so that it thickens. Pat the salmon dry with kitchen paper and lightly oil the fillets on both sides. Heat a heavy-based frying pan then put the salmon in, skin side down. Cook for 3 - 4 minutes, brushing with the marinade halfway through. Turn the fish over and baste again, squeezing over the lime juice and cook for a further 2 - 3 minutes or so depending on thickness so that it has just turned opaque in the centre.

Meanwhile, heat a tablespoon of oil in a frying pan or wok and toss in the spring onions, garlic and pak choi and stir-fry, with another dash of the marinade, for a few minutes until wilted.

To serve, divide the vegetables between the plates and sit the salmon on top with the crispy skin side uppermost. Drizzle over any remaining marinade.

Tips
FROM THE SINK

- A salmon tail, as opposed to individual fillets, is also excellent cooked thus.

MUSHROOMS AND COD

The virtue of this is that it is wonderfully quick and straightforward.

- 4 cod fillets, skinned
- Squeeze lemon juice
- 50g / 2 oz butter
- 50g / 8 oz white mushrooms, peeled and thinly sliced
- 2 tbsp dill leaves, chopped
- Pinch or two of Aromat
- Olive oil
- 300ml / ½ pint double cream

Preheat the oven to 180 C. Remove any bones from the fish and squeeze over the lemon juice then rub the dill and Aromat onto the fish. Melt the butter in a pan and fry the mushrooms until soft.

Cook the cod in olive oil in a large non-stick frying pan for approximately 5 minutes, turning halfway through until the flesh is bright white. Transfer to a warmed serving dish.

Meanwhile, heat the cream in a pan, add the mushrooms, check seasoning and when very hot, spoon around the fish. Serve immediately.

YUMPSH COD
(SERVES 6)

Rosie Clark dishes this up with her trademark style and panache. Her dinners are, of course, matched by the excellence of her husband's cellar. Haynes, Hanson & Clark - of which Nick is Managing Director - are amongst the finest independent wine merchants offering interesting hand-picked wines from well-sourced vineyards. Within their extensive list, they are also especially famed for their outstanding selection of Burgundian wines.

- 750g / 1 ½ lbs mashed potato (See page 123)
- 2 tbsp olive oil
- 4 spring onions, white part only, finely sliced
- 750g / 1 ½ lbs spinach leaves, cooked and drained
- 6 cod portions, square cut and skinned
- 75g / 3 oz butter
- Juice ½ lemon
- Sprinkling sea salt and freshly ground black pepper

Sauce:

- ½ fish stock cube
- 200g / 6 oz cold butter, cut into small cubes
- 2 tbsp double cream
- Squeeze lemon juice
- Seasoning
- Finely scissored chives, to decorate

Take the mashed potato (which must be hot) and beat in the olive oil, then mix in the spring onions and keep warm. Place the cooked spinach in a dish and keep warm also.

Preheat the oven to 200 C. Butter an ovenproof dish and place the cod fillets in this together with 2 tbsp cold water, the lemon juice and sprinkle on sea salt and the pepper. Put a nut of butter on each piece of cod and cook for 6 minutes until white and opaque. Meanwhile, make the sauce by putting 150ml / ¼ pint boiling water in a saucepan with the fish stock cube. When simmering, gradually whisk in the butter a few cubes at a time followed by the double cream, lemon juice to taste and seasoning.

To serve, divide the mashed potatoes between 6 preheated plates, arrange the spinach on top followed by the fish. Spoon over creamy sauce and finish off with a scattering of chives on each one.

MIGHTY MUSSELS

I love this dish. In essence, it's a Thai-style Moules Marinières with a lot more power and depth of flavour. You can tinker with the flavourings as you see fit - for instance, you might want to include crushed garlic and some stalks of lemongrass too - but I have tried to avoid a list of 995 ingredients here!

- 2 kg / 4 ½ lbs fresh mussels – make sure they are good quality
- Bunch spring onions, white parts only, finely chopped
- Small cube root ginger, peeled, squashed and finely chopped
- Red chilli, seeded and cut into slivers
- 2 x 400ml / 14 fl oz tins coconut milk
- Zest and juice of a lime
- Tbsp soft brown sugar
- Shake of Nam Pla (Thai fish sauce)
- 3 tbsp coriander leaves, chopped

Begin by washing the mussels thoroughly, scrubbing off any barnacles and pulling away any beards. Change the water and rinse well. If any are open at this stage, tap them firmly and if they don't close immediately, then discard. Put the spring onions, ginger and chilli into a large pan and add a little of the coconut milk and cook over a medium heat until everything is soft. Add the rest of the milk, the lime zest and juice, sugar and fish sauce. Bring almost to the boil and then tip in the mussels. Give the pan a good shake, cover with a lid and cook for approx 4 minutes or until the mussels have opened. To serve, stir them around in their liquid then scatter on the coriander leaves and serve immediately with warmed baguette to mop up all those juices.

Tips FROM THE SINK

- You can rev this up by adding cooked pasta such as tagliatelle, squid ink taglioni or even those dinky little pasta bows or, if you prefer, rice.

SEA BASS FILLETS WITH SAUCE VIERGE

- 4 fillets sea bass, skin on and scaled
- Tbsp olive oil
- Few nuts of butter
- Lemon, sliced
- Handful fresh herb stalks, i.e. parsley, tarragon, dill
- 2 - 3 lemongrass stalks, slit in half lengthways
- Seasoning
- Splash white wine or water

Sauce Vierge:

- 3 large ripe, flavoursome vine or plum tomatoes, skinned (page 228)
- 150ml / ¼ pint olive oil
- Tbsp each basil, tarragon and flat-leaf parsley leaves, chopped
- Juice of ½ lemon
- Seasoning

Make the sauce ahead. Cut the skinned tomatoes into quarters, discarding the seeds, and finely dice the flesh. Put into a bowl and mix in the olive oil, herbs, lemon juice and seasoning. This keeps very well in the fridge for up to two weeks and also goes well with salads, other fish such as tuna and with chicken and lamb dishes.

Preheat the oven to 190 C. Lay a very large sheet of tin foil on the base of a baking sheet (leaving enough overhang so that you can bring the sides up to fold over and overlap). Check the fish for any bones and remove these with a pair of tweezers. Place the fillets on the tin foil and pour around the oil. Dot over the butter, lemon slices, herbs, lemongrass and season. Add the white wine or water then fold up the tin foil to make a loose but secure parcel. Bake in the oven for approximately 12 - 15 minutes until the fish is white and opaque and just firm to the touch. Remove from the oven and serve with the Sauce Vierge.

BATSFORD BOUILLABAISSE
(SERVES 12 - 15)

Catering for large numbers has never been my bag and, as a rule of thumb, is something I have always avoided. On one occasion, however, I was press-ganged into this very role but all for a very good charitable cause. 120 paying guests and hungry mouths to feed in the great Ballroom at Batsford House was a daunting prospect for a girl geared to cooking for a maximum of twelve friends. It would have to be a one-stop, one-pot dish so I devised my own version of that much celebrated and highly revered Bouillabaisse found on the Cote d'Azur. How to recreate this dish at home? You cannot duplicate it - but, with the help of a good fishmonger who will also prepare the fish for you - a perfectly delicious interpretation can be brought to the table.

- 150ml / 6 fl oz olive oil
- 300g / 10 oz onions, peeled and chopped
- 250g / 8 oz leeks, trimmed washed and chopped
- 2 heads of fennel, trimmed and chopped
- 4 garlic cloves, peeled and minced
- 2 bay leaves
- Bouquet garni
- 2 x 400g tins chopped tomatoes
- 4 tbsp tomato purée
- ½ bottle dry white wine
- ½ bottle Noilly Prat
- 600 ml / 1 pint fish stock
- Seasoning
- 2 ½ kg / 5 lbs mixed fish to include - salmon, monkfish, haddock and cod - (skinned and boned, cut into bite-sized pieces), plus mussels (well scrubbed), shelled raw prawns and lobster claws
- 500g / 1 lb small new potatoes, cooked
- Juice 2 lemons
- 12 - 15 langoustine, shell on, cooked
- 2 tbsp each flat-leaf parsley, basil, tarragon and dill, leaves only, finely chopped
- 2 pots French rouille
- Aioli (page 215)
- French bread, sliced and toasted - to make croûtes

Fish

Take a gargantuan pan, pour in the olive oil and heat through then add the onions, leeks, fennel, garlic and cook gently until softened. Add the bay leaves, bouquet garni, tomatoes, tomato purée, white wine, Noilly Prat and fish stock and bring everything to a simmer. Cook for at least 20 minutes.

Approximately 15 minutes before you are ready to eat, add all the fish, bar the langoustine, and cook in the sauce. Do not allow this to 'stew' so keep a careful eye on it. Tip in the potatoes so that they will heat through. Taste the sauce and add as much lemon juice as necessary. Check seasoning and stir in one pot of the rouille. Stir in the herbs keeping a few back for the garnish.

To serve, ladle into large preheated soup dishes or similar. Top each one with a langoustine, add a few more herbs and bring to the table. Hand round the other pot of rouille, the aioli and the toasted croûtes.

FISH WITH GREEN MASALA

You can use any white fish fillets and I have also made this with salmon.

Masala Paste:

- Large bunch coriander
- Good chunk root ginger, peeled and roughly chopped
- 2 garlic cloves, peeled and crushed
- Green chilli, finely sliced
- Juice of a lime
- Handful cumin seeds, toasted and finely ground
- Seasoning

- 2 tbsp plain yoghurt
- 4 fish fillets, skin on
- Olive or sunflower oil
- Lime wedges, to serve

Blend the first six ingredients together in a food processor to a wet green paste, then season. Toss the fish in half the mixture. Heat a griddle or non-stick pan and add a little oil then cook the fish skin side up for approx 7 – 8 minutes. Alternatively, preheat the oven to 180 and bake the fish with oil for around 12 minutes, depending on thickness of the fillets.

To serve, mix the yoghurt with the remaining paste to make a sauce and spoon over the fish. Add wedges of lime to squeeze over.

TRAY-BAKED
FISH 'N' RAINBOW VEG

An easy all-in-one dish for suppers and dinners, quick and simple to prepare. Any white fish fillets can be used for this – i.e. sole, plaice, sea bass, bream, pollack etc.

- 4 lemon sole fillets, or other white fish
- Assortment of vegetables to include:
  - Red pepper
  - Yellow pepper
  - 2 courgettes
  - Aubergine
  - 2 red onions
  - Bunch spring onions
  - 300g / 10 oz red and yellow cherry tomatoes
  - Handful new potatoes, parboiled
  - Few garlic cloves, peeled and chopped (optional)
- 2 - 3 tbsp olive oil
- Juice ½ lemon plus extra for fish
- Few nuts of butter
- Seasoning
- Black olives
- Flat-leaf parsley or basil leaves, chopped or torn

Preheat oven to 190 C. Begin by prepping the vegetables. Seed and slice peppers and onions. Cut courgettes and aubergine into discs. Trim and chop spring onions and put all in a baking tray. Add the cherry tomatoes and parboiled potatoes and pour on the oil and lemon juice, then season well. Roast the vegetables for at least 35 minutes until all are soft and lightly coloured. Remove from the oven and set aside until you are ready to cook the fish – i.e. when the first course is on to the table!

Throw the olives into the vegetable dish, then sit the fish fillets on top, seasoning each one and dotting with little nuts of butter and a spritz more lemon juice. Cover with tin foil and return to the oven for approx 12 - 15 minutes until the fish is white and opaque. Scatter on the herbs and bring to the table as is.

FISH IN NEWSPAPER

This is a fun way of cooking fish and ensures it remains nice and juicy. It's also a great way of barbequing fish and works equally well for a large salmon, particularly if you don't own a fish kettle.

- Yesterday's newspaper, preferably broadsheet
- 4 individual whole fish - i.e. sea bream, sea bass, cleaned and gutted
- Lemon wedges
- Handful assorted herbs, i.e. dill, parsley, tarragon
- Seasoning
- Lemon quarters, to serve

Preheat the oven to 190 - 200 C. Using the blade of a sharp knife, roughly scale the fish. Stuff the belly cavity with the lemon wedges and a handful of herbs. Season the fish and then wrap in 3 - 4 pages of newspaper which has been run under the tap. Grease a large baking sheet and place the fish on it and bake until the newspaper has dried out completely. Then the fish will be ready. To serve, simply peel off the paper, as well as the skin, and transfer to a platter and sit some lemon wedges around.

Poultry

The golden rule about poultry, and chicken in particular, is uber simple. The better the bird, the better the dish cooked. Factory-reared chickens are an abomination - one only has to look at their conditions to realise that the chances of producing anything edible from such scrawnbags are impossible. Pumped full of artificial food and water in an attempt to make them plump, they are quite without flavour and the texture of their flesh resembles cotton wool. However brilliant a cook one may be, they will only ever disappoint.

A free-range bird, on the other hand, reared in favourable conditions and properly hung to maximise its flavour, is a delight. In an ideal world it will come complete with giblets and liver - the former is good for the stockpot or gravy whilst the latter can be turned into paté (page 49). Such a chicken is always a source of joy. Apply the same rule of thumb also when choosing your Christmas turkey.

ROAST CHICKEN

Is there really anything to equal a roast chicken? I can honestly say it is right up there amongst my favourite foods. Some cooks advocate cooking it sitting on its back, others put it in the pan lying on one side and then the other. For me, it just needs to be glorious, golden and deliciously impressive. When treated properly, it delights with its juicy, almost silken flesh. So, cosset and nurture your bird and, above all, cook it with love. Oh, and plenty of butter.

- 100g / 4 oz butter, softened
- 1.8 - 2 kg / 4 lb + free-range chicken
- Seasoning - try the Herbed Sea Salt (page 226)
- Lemon
- Sprigs of thyme, rosemary and/or tarragon
- 2 tbsp olive oil
- Splash white wine or stock

Preheat the oven to 200 C. Sit the bird in a roasting tray which allows room for basting purposes. Smear the butter all over the bird and season well then squeeze over the juice from the lemon and put the two halves inside the cavity of the bird along with the herbs. Pour on the olive oil and tip the white wine / stock into the base of the tin. Roast in the oven for 10 - 15 minutes then remove and baste thoroughly.

Reduce the temperature to 180 C and roast for a further 40 - 45 minutes, basting every 10 - 15 minutes. The bird should be golden brown all over with a crispy skin. Remove from the oven and leave, covered with tin foil, in a warm place for a further 15 minutes to allow it to rest. This is vital as it enables the flesh to relax which makes carving far easier.

The juices in the base of the pan only need a light whisk and should then be strained before serving.

WHOLE POACHED CHICKEN

Thanks to Simon Hopkinson, this has become one of my favourite ways of cooking a bird retaining, as it does, a wonderful juicy tenderness within the flesh. Take a meaty young chicken and a fresh, as opposed to frozen, one. Prepare a large pot of simmering water to which you have added a couple of bay leaves, a few knobs of root ginger, a slick of sherry and salt. Immerse the chicken in the liquid making sure it is entirely covered and put the lid on the pot and cook gently (so that just the odd 'blip' of water breaks the surface of the liquid) for at least two and a half hours, then remove from the stove and leave to stand until completely cold before removing from its broth.

Simon recommends a more sophisticated way of simmering the bird for a few minutes at a time, then removing it from the heat and allowing it so steep for about half an hour, before repeating the process repeatedly. Since, however, I am usually trying to garden or do something away from the kitchen, I have found my method, as above, works equally satisfactorily.

Remove the skin then strip the flesh from the carcass (keep this for the stockpot) and proceed with your chosen receipt. I particularly like using chicken cooked in this way for salads dressed, perhaps, with Tarragon Cream Sauce (page 219) or to make Bang-Bang Chicken (on following page).

BANG-BANG CHICKEN

(SERVES 5 - 6)

Come summer when one wants a fail-safe chicken dish, this one turns up trumps. And whilst I have a certain loyalty to Coronation Chicken, it does tend to get trotted out rather too frequently for my liking. Bang-Bang has therefore been promoted though it is no good for anyone with a nut allergy!

- Large, fresh free-range chicken, poached (page 81)
- 2 tbsp granulated sugar
- 4 tbsp rice vinegar
- Tsp salt
- 2 - 3 carrots, peeled and cut into thin matchsticks
- Cucumber, peeled, seeded and cut into thin batons
- Bunch spring onions, white part only, thinly sliced
- 250g / 8 oz sugar snap peas, blanched thinly sliced
- 250g / 8 oz bean sprouts
- 2 little gem or cos lettuce, chopped crossways
- Bunch watercress, thick stems removed
- 75g / 3 oz peanuts
- Tbsp each mint and coriander leaves, chopped
- Tbsp sesame seeds, lightly toasted

Sauce:

- 5 tbsp smooth peanut butter
- 3 tsp sweet chilli jam
- 2 tbsp toasted sesame oil
- Shake soy sauce

Strip the flesh from the chicken and set aside, keeping the carcass for the stockpot.

Heat the sugar, vinegar and salt in a saucepan to dissolve and then simmer until syrupy before pouring over the prepared vegetables.

For the sauce, combine the ingredients in a saucepan over a low heat and mix well - or stand a bowl on the Aga top and leave to warm through.

To assemble, cover the base of a large plate or dish with the lettuce then pile on the vegetables, followed by the chicken and the watercress. Pour over the sauce then top with the peanuts, herbs and sesame seeds.

SANGRIA CHICKEN

This is strictly seasonal relying, as it does, on the brief appearance in January of blood oranges - but it's well worth the wait to tease and titillate the palate and it is so easy.

- 6 blood oranges
- Juice of a lemon
- 3 tbsp dark brown sugar
- 4 tbsp olive oil
- 150ml / 5 fl oz fino sherry
- Tbsp Dijon mustard
- 8 boneless free-range chicken thighs, skin on
- 2 plump fennel bulbs, trimmed and thinly sliced
- Tbsp fresh thyme leaves

Zest and juice two of the oranges and slice the other four into thin rounds, about 1 cm thickness. In a bowl, mix the orange zest and juice together with the lemon juice, sugar, oil, sherry and mustard as a marinade.

Place the chicken thighs, fennel and orange slices plus the thyme into a roasting dish or tray, then pour over the marinade. Cover and leave overnight in the fridge.

Preheat the oven to 200 C and cook the chicken for an hour, basting from time to time, until the juices run clear and the skin is brown and crisp. Drain off the fat and pour the remaining cooking liquid into a pan and boil to reduce then return to the original dish. I serve this with waxy new potatoes and purple-sprouting broccoli.

COQ AU VIN
(SERVES 6)

This invariably excites great discussion as to how, precisely, it should be made and there are an almost limitless number of different receipts. Miles Morland, who lives on a boat in Chelsea, is not only a financial whizz, a captivating author, an adventure/adrenaline junky, avid motorbike rider and traveller but he also happens to be a terrific cook. He insists the secret ingredients here are black treacle and coffee. After all, an original Coq au Vin would have included a healthy splash of the cockerel's blood which isn't something most of us can lay our hands on today. The key to this dish is that it must be made several days in advance. It also freezes well.

- Large free-range chicken, jointed – approx 2 - 2 ¾ kgs / 4 ½ - 5 lbs
- Bottle decent red wine
- 2 bay leaves
- Few sprigs fresh thyme
- 2 garlic cloves, crushed
- Olive oil
- Lump of butter
- Litre / 2.2 pints homemade chicken stock (best supermarket tubs of fresh are fine but they aren't a patch on your own!)

Marinade:

- Large leek, cleaned and sliced
- 2 carrots, roughly chopped
- 2 shallots, diced
- Salt and pepper
- Olive oil

To finish the dish:

- 100g / 4 oz button mushrooms
- 100g / 4 oz baby onions (see Tip from the Sink)
- 100g / 4 oz streaky bacon, diced
- Tbsp black treacle
- Tsp instant coffee
- 4 slices white bread, crusts removed
- Olive oil
- Tbsp flat-leaf parsley, chopped

Trim chicken joints of any excess fat, leaving skin on. Season with salt and pepper and set aside. Put the bottle of red wine into a pan together with the herbs and garlic, and bring to the boil then reduce the heat and simmer until the liquid is reduced by half. Cool and then add to the chicken stock with the marinade vegetables. Pour over the chicken, cover and leave in a cold place overnight.

Next, remove the chicken from the marinade and pat dry. Heat the oil in a pan and fry the chicken pieces, a few at a time, until golden brown on all sides. Don't be tempted to hurl the whole lot into the casserole in one go as they need time and space so that the flavour intensifies.

When this is complete, return all to the casserole dish. Pour the liquid and vegetables back over it and bring everything to the boil. Cover with a tight fitting lid, then place in the oven at a low temperature at around 150 C for at least 2 hours. Meanwhile, put the well rinsed onions into a heavy pan with some olive oil and butter, and sauté until they begin to colour then fry the bacon / lardons until cooked.

Once the chicken is tender, remove from the dish and strain the sauce, pressing hard on the vegetables. Return the strained sauce to the pan and boil to reduce until it thickens slightly. Add the treacle and instant coffee and stir in well followed by the onions, bacon / lardons and the mushrooms. Replace the chicken and simmer to warm through thoroughly.

Garnish the dish by cutting the bread into triangles and frying these off with some oil / butter in the onion and bacon pan. Arrange these on top of the Coq and sprinkle over the parsley.

Tips FROM THE SINK

- I buy a jar of baby onions from the supermarket and rinse thoroughly in cold running water to get rid of the briney flavour. It saves all that sobbing whilst peeling.

CHRISTMAS TURKEY

'How do you cook yours?' is an oft repeated and asked question in the run-up to Christmas. There are, of course, a hundred different ways and none of them are wrong. Indeed every cook swears by their own tried and tested method to produce the perfect bird, succulent and tender. One year, I circulated the following mantra which won approval from those on turkey duty.

Preheat the oven to 200 C. Take your free-range turkey (I usually buy one which weighs around 7 kgs / 14 - 15 lbs) and bring to room temperature. Remove the giblets, neck and liver etc from the cavity of the bird and boil these up with some water as the base for your gravy. Strain and set aside. If you are putting stuffing inside, then do so now before covering the surface of the bird with softened butter, salt and freshly ground better. Sit in a large baking tray big enough to get a large spoon into the sides with ease in order to baste frequently. Pour in a little white wine or stock just so that it can create a steam effect.

Toss in some herbs such as thyme and rosemary and a few roughly chopped onions, un-peeled, for extra flavour. Cover the turkey with strong tin foil, allowing some room inside (i.e. not too tightly) and seal securely round the sides of the tin. Cook in the oven for the first 45 minutes and then lower the temperature to 180 C and continue to cook for another 2 hours, basting the bird as frequently as you can. For the last 25 minutes or so, remove the foil and brush the skin with warmed maple syrup or honey and allow the skin to brown. Remove from the oven and transfer to a warmed serving platter, cover and leave to stand in a warm place. It will retain its heat for ages and needs to rest so that the meat can relax before carving.

For the gravy, drain off the cooking juices and set to one side, discarding the fat. Put a tablespoon of flour into the baking tin, and gradually add the reserved giblet stock (strained) followed by the cooking juices, whisking or stirring thoroughly as you go. Spritz up with a little white or red wine, some redcurrant jelly, seasoning and a squeeze of lemon juice. Prior to bringing to the table, pour any cooking juices that have collected on the platter into the gravy.

SLOW-COOKED CHINESE DUCK LEGS

I have no shame in admitting that this dish makes a frequent appearance at my table. It is reliable, and can, indeed must, be prepared in advance which is music to my ears and everyone always clamours for the receipt. What's not to like?

- 4 duck legs
- 2 large tsp Chinese five-spice powder
- Salt
- 150ml / 1/4 pint water
- 2 tbsp soy sauce (dark or light)
- Glass of sherry
- Tbsp sweet chilli sauce
- Tbsp honey
- Cube root ginger, peeled and finely chopped
- 2 garlic cloves, peeled and crushed
- 2 star anise

Preheat the oven to 170 C. Rub the duck legs all over with the five-spice powder and salt. Heat a dry heavy-based frying pan or casserole and add the legs, skin side down. Brown very well, turn over and repeat the exercise. Remove these from the pan and pour off the fat and discard. Return the pan to the heat and add the remaining ingredients and stir to combine then put the duck legs back in plus any juices. Bring to the boil, cover with a lid and cook in the oven for at least 1 1/2 hours. I often cook mine for longer by moving them down to the bottom right hand oven of my two-door Aga. Leave to cool then refrigerate and remove the fat which has solidified on the surface the following day. Take out the duck legs, heat up the sauce and reduce well. To serve, return the duck to the pan and heat through. Noodles mixed with stir-fry vegetables and finished off with a snowstorm of chopped coriander leaves are the perfect accompaniment.

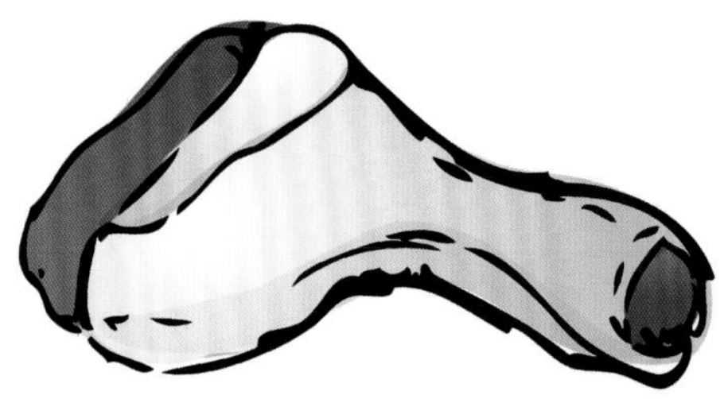

DUCK WITH CRANBERRY, STAR ANISE & ORANGE SAUCE WITH ROASTED SWEET POTATOES

3 large magret de canard, skin scored in lattice pattern and seasoned.

Sauce:

- 300g fresh cranberries
- 2 tbsp sugar
- Zest and juice of an orange
- Glass red wine
- 8 - 10 star anise
- Seasoning

- 4 - 5 medium-sized sweet potatoes
- 2 - 3 tbsp olive oil
- Salt and black pepper

Preheat the oven to 190 - 200 C. Peel the potatoes, cut in half and then into quarters lengthways and slice crossways to make cubes. Toss in a bowl together with the olive oil and seasoning and turn into a baking tray. Roast in the oven for approx 35 minutes. (Can be done ahead and simply reheated).

To make the sauce, which can also be done well ahead and freezes very well, simply tip the cranberries into a saucepan together with the other ingredients and simmer gently over the heat until the liquid has reduced and the mixture is jammy but still quite runny. Remove the star anise as they could bring the evening to a standstill if stuck in the throat!

Preheat the oven to 200 C and cook the duck by placing the breasts on a rack, skin side up, and cook in the oven for 12 - 15 minutes until they are nicely browned on top. Remove and keep warm.

To serve, slice the duck breasts into thin slivers diagonally then place on a warmed serving dish and spoon over the sauce. Arrange the potato around the edge of the plate.

Tips
FROM THE SINK

- Roasted squash makes a delicious alternative to sweet potato and is wonderful when mixed with some cooked lentils and stir-fried pak choy.

Game

If poets and cuckoos welcome the advent of spring, then sportsmen rejoice as autumn approaches. After all, the season of mist and mellow fruitfulness also marks the start of the game season. In addition to grouse shooting (pray the young birds have survived the wet which invariably threatens them soon after they have hatched) so that the 'Purple Office', as it is fondly known, can open with record numbers; there is stalking, duck flighting to mention nothing of partridge, pheasant and, in boggy areas, woodcock and snipe to bag for the pot.

The familiar challenge when handling any type of game is to find new ways in which to present it at the table, whilst retaining its own distinctive flavour. In my book there are but two basic rules to remember when dealing with feathered game. First, the younger the bird the more tender the result is likely to be, and the less you will have to do to it; but for plain roasting purposes - trussing, barding, larding and basting, followed by more basting will pay dividends to the end result. Second, don't bother cooking old birds!

HAUNCH OF VENISON
(SERVES 8)

Venison is by nature a very lean meat so it needs to be cooked with care in order not to dry out. Marinating it well before and wrapping it up during cooking will ensure it remains juicy.

Marinade:

- Generous half bottle red wine
- 6 tbsp olive oil
- Handful juniper berries, crushed
- Zest and juice of an orange
- Herb stalks such as thyme, rosemary and parsley
- 2 bay leaves, crumbled
- 4 garlic cloves, peeled and finely sliced
- Freshly ground black pepper and sea salt

- Haunch of venison, on the bone (approx 4 -5 kgs / 8 - 10+ lbs)
- 2 tbsp butter, softened

Mix the marinade ingredients together and place in a large dish together with the joint. Cover and leave in a cold place for at least 24 hours (48 would be preferable) turning the meat over periodically and basting with the liquid.

To cook, preheat the oven to 190 – 200 C. Take a very large sheet of tin foil and spread with the softened butter. Place in a large baking tray and lay the venison in the centre of this. Pour over the marinade then seal the parcel up firmly, allowing it room inside to steam. Cook in the oven for at least 1 ½ - 1 ¾ hours. To check when ready, insert a sharp knife into the meat – if it glides in and the joint feels tender, then it is done. Remove from the heat, leave wrapped in the foil parcel and allow to rest for at least 45 minutes.

Serve with gravy and strain in the remaining cooking juices. I often add the remains of a bottle of homemade sloe vodka to mine.

VENISON CARPACCIO
(SERVES 6)

Named after the Venetian painter, Vittore Carpaccio, this dish is traditionally made using fillet of beef. With venison available all year round, this makes a worthy alternative. The paper-thin elegance of the slices makes it look strikingly good on a plate, especially when decorated with zig-zags of its accompanying sauce *(page 217)**.*

- 300g / 10 oz red deer fillet or roe deer loin
- Seasoning
- Olive oil
- Rocket leaves

Set a plate in the fridge ready for slicing. Trim the venison, ensuring to remove any silver skin and season all over. Heat oil in a hot pan then sear the venison briefly and evenly resulting in a thin brown crust all over. Remove from the heat and allow to rest before wrapping tightly in cling film as for a ballotine to ensure a tightly rolled barrel. Set in the freezer to chill for 2 hours before slicing. When ready to slice, unwrap and slice immediately into wafer-thin slices against the grain, placing on the chilled plate until ready to serve. If you are nervous of achieving transparently thin slices, then cut these a little thicker and beat each piece out between two sheets of cling film. Always serve at room temperature. Garnish with a few rocket leaves and the sauce.

PARTRIDGE WITH PEARS

A straightforward way of cooking these birds. If you happen to have a terracotta chicken 'brick' so much the better as these do seal in the flavour. Remember to soak both parts of the brick in advance for a couple of hours filled with cold water. If no brick, an ordinary casserole dish with a lid is fine.

- 4 partridge
- 4 - 5 pears, quartered and cored, skin on
- 4 shallots, peeled and halved (I use banana shallots)
- 300ml / ½ pint cider or perry
- 2 bay leaves

Preheat the oven to 200 C. Place the birds in the brick or casserole with the pears, cider / perry, shallots and bay leaves and cook, covered, for 30 minutes. Remove the lid and check the birds are cooked though. To finish, remove the partridge and keep them warm. Boil up the cider / perry to reduce slightly, check seasoning and then return the birds to the dish. Serve with creamy Mashed Potatoes or Celeriac Dauphinoise (pages 123 and 121 respectively).

THAI SHITAKE PHEASANT
(SERVES 4 - 5)

A departure from the routine pheasant receipts. This prep-ahead dish is a great one to have up your sleeve. The pheasant breasts are carved before the final cooking which saves any last minute labour.

- Tbsp sunflower oil
- 300g / 10 oz shitake mushrooms, sliced
- Seasoning
- Tbsp Thai red curry paste
- Tbsp tamarind paste
- 400ml / ¾ pint coconut milk
- Tbsp Nam Pla (Thai fish sauce)
- Juice and zest of 2 limes
- Tbsp soft brown sugar
- Tbsp cornflour, slaked in a little coconut milk
- 4 pheasant breasts, skin removed
- Bunch of fresh basil or coriander, chopped

Preheat the oven to 200 C. Heat the oil in a non-stick frying pan, add the mushrooms and fry over a high heat for a few minutes. Season and when cooked, scatter over the base of a large, shallow ovenproof dish. To the same pan, add the Thai paste, tamarind paste, coconut milk, fish sauce, lime juice and zest plus the sugar. Bring to the boil for a few minutes and season to taste. Add a little hot sauce to the cornflour paste and tip this into the pan, stirring continuously while bringing back to the boil so that it thickens.

Cut each pheasant breast in three widthways, then place on top of the mushrooms and pour over the sauce when ready to cook but not before. Bake in the oven for 20 - 30 minutes. I like to serve this with rice, chutney (page 201) and perhaps a cucumber and mint raita plus poppadoms.

Tips FROM THE SINK

- There will be some sauce leftover so either freeze it or reheat and serve with prawns.

Game

GAME PUDDING

Suet pastry:

- 300g / 12 oz self-raising flour
- 150g / 6 oz shredded (beef) suet
- 200 - 225 ml / 7 fl oz cold water
- Salt
- Thyme leaves

Pudding:

- 500g / 1 lb assorted game, i.e. venison, partridge, pheasant, grouse and rabbit, roughly cubed and tossed in seasoned flour
- Olive oil
- Onion or 2 shallots, finely chopped
- 2 sticks celery, finely sliced
- Flour
- Red wine or Madeira
- 100g / 4 oz pitted prunes
- Bouquet garni
- Game stock to cover
- Seasoning

In a large bowl, mix suet through the flour with salt and thyme and add water to make a paste then roughly knead and roll out in more flour. Line a greased basin (3 pint capacity) or individual bowls with ¾ of the pastry, leaving plenty of overlap.

For the pudding itself, using a large cast iron or heavy-based pan, fry off the onions/shallots and celery in the oil until softened then remove with a slotted spoon and set aside. Add a little more oil and briefly brown the meat in batches until all is done. Blend the flour into the remaining meat juices then add the alcohol, onion mixture, prunes, bouquet garni, stock and seasoning. Ladle into the pudding basin(s), fold the overhang of the lining pastry over the top of the filling and, using some water or milk, sealing a lid with the remaining pastry onto each one. Cover with cling film then bring to the boil in a large pan or bain-marie. Place tin foil over the entire surface and steam for 2 ½ hours (or less if making smaller-sized puddings) then leave to stand before turning out.

Tips FROM THE SINK

- If the thought of making the suet crust puts you off, then simply go ahead and cook the game as for a casserole and turn into an ovenproof pie dish and top with puff pastry and cook until golden brown.

NICK'S WAYS WITH GROUSE & PARTRIDGE

Be it grouse, partridge, pheasant, duck or the more elusive woodcock, snipe or pigeon - Nick is very adept at cooking such birds having despatched them with equal skill. As we all know, they have a general tendency to dry out unless carefully handled.

Preheat the oven to 200 C. A modest amount of softened butter is rubbed onto the breast of the very young grouse or partridge which is then seasoned. Wrap each bird individually in aluminium foil and put the parcels in a baking tin and into the oven to cook for 20 minutes. Then undo the foil and return the birds to the oven for a further 5 minutes. Remove and leave to rest, loosely covered, in a warm place for 15 minutes before serving together with the classic accompaniments which include game chips, breadcrumbs and bread sauce.*

Another successful method is to put softened butter between the skin and flesh of the birds. Place salt and half a peeled onion into their cavities, wrap with streaky bacon and roast in the oven at 200 C for 15 minutes, basting once or twice. To serve, cut off the breasts and arrange these on a large platter on top of cooked green cabbage, leeks and onions.

** Nick never cooks birds shot after the end of August as by then they have already started to become tough.*

PIGEON AND HEDGEROW SALAD

Although pigeon has no close season, I like to serve this in the autumn when the blackberry bushes are laden with fruit and waiting to be picked for the enjoyment of cooks and diners alike. Since the breasts are the only part of a pigeon which are edible, don't bother with plucking these birds. Simply skin them down the middle and lift out the breasts.

- 4 pigeon breasts, skin removed
- 2 tbsp olive oil
- Seasoning

Dressing:

- 3 tbsp olive oil
- 2 tsp Dijon mustard
- Tbsp cider vinegar
- Tbsp chives, finely chopped

Salad:

- 50g / 2 oz blanched hazelnuts (available in packets)
- 4 handfuls mixed salad leaves
- 100g / 4 oz blackberries

Toss the pigeon breasts in the olive oil and season well on both sides then set aside.

To make the dressing, mix the oil, mustard and vinegar with the chives and add a little water.

Heat a dry frying pan and toast the nuts until golden then remove and set aside.

Return the pan to the heat and fry the pigeon breasts for 2 - 3 minutes on each side, then leave to rest in the pan for 5 minutes.

To serve, divide the salad leaves between 4 plates and add the nuts and blackberries. Thinly slice the pigeon breasts and arrange on top then pour on a little dressing. Dress with extra chives if wished.

WILD DUCK
(SERVES 2 - 3)

Their dark, close-knit flesh is a far cry from that of a farmyard duck. Unless one takes care, however, they can end up being a dry, old affair but this receipt produces a delectable result.

- 2 wild duck
- 25g / 1 oz butter
- 2 tbsp oil
- 4 tbsp Marsala
- 2 tbsp tomato purée
- 2 tbsp potato flour
- 450ml / ¾ pint chicken stock
- Seasoning
- Bay leaf
- 75g / 3 oz mushrooms, sliced
- Red pimento, diced
- Zest of an orange
- Orange, peeled, pith removed and segmented
- 3 tomatoes, skinned and sliced (page 228)
- Bunch watercress

Joint the ducks into pieces (a friendly butcher will do this for you, especially if he has plucked it for you) and brown all over in a casserole with the butter and oil. Pour on the Marsala then remove the ducks from the pan and add the tomato purée and flour. Stir to a roux and then gradually pour on the stock stirring continuously. Return the birds and add the bay leaf and simmer for 45 minutes. Put the mushrooms, pimento, orange zest and segments plus the sliced tomatoes in a separate pan and cook very gently. When the ducks are cooked, remove them from the gravy and reduce to thicken if necessary then pour in the orange mixture. Check seasoning. Pour the sauce over the ducks, garnish with watercress and serve.

ROAST WOODCOCK

Of all the varieties of game, woodcock is a very prized species; not least because they are such an elusive bird. Strictly speaking, they should be served ungutted and every morsel, including their brain, devoured. Not for the faint-hearted then. Allow them to hang for around 3 days before cooking. For serious devotees, cold woodcock served for breakfast are considered the ultimate delicacy.

- 4 woodcock
- 100g / 4 oz butter, melted
- Seasoning
- 8 rashers streaky bacon
- 5 fl oz / 100 ml brandy
- 4 pieces decent white bread, crusts removed and toasted on one side only

Preheat the oven to 190 C. Brush the woodcock with the melted butter and season well. Wrap 2 rashers of bacon around each bird. Sit in a roasting tin and cook in the oven for around 15 - 18 minutes (rare or medium). Place one piece of the half toasted bread (cooked side down) under each bird 5 minutes into the cooking time to catch the trail as it drops out. Before the birds are done, remove the bacon and baste each woodcock, then return to the oven to brown.

Remove from the heat, transfer to a heated plate and cover to keep warm. Place the roasting tin back on the stove over a high heat, pour over the brandy and warm through then set it alight. Let the flames die out and serve at once. A simple accompaniment of watercress and game chips (homemade if you want to be posh) is all that is necessary.

RABBIT TERRINE

(SERVES 6)

Wild rabbits tend to be tough but flavoursome whereas tame ones are fleshy with pale pinky-white meat. Any good rabbit, however - whether wild or tame - will produce a fine terrine. I am particularly fond of this receipt as it not too high and gamey but, equally, it does have flavour.

- 300g / 10 oz rabbit loin, boned
- 100g / 4 oz pork back fat
- 300g / 10 oz skinless pork belly
- 75g / 3 oz pork fillet
- 4 rashers streaky bacon, rinds removed
- 100 ml / 3 ½ fl oz brandy or amontillado sherry
- 3 shallots, peeled and finely diced
- 3 garlic cloves, peeled and finely chopped
- 50g / 2 oz butter
- Egg, beaten
- Tsp dried mixed herbs
- 2 tbsp fresh breadcrumbs
- 100 ml 3 ½ fl oz Port or brandy
- 50g / oz pistachio nuts, dry toasted
- Tbsp green peppercorns, drained
- 5 - 6 juniper berries, crushed
- Seasoning

Preheat the oven to 170 C. Neatly dice the rabbit meat and whizz the leg meat, pork meat, fat and bacon in a food processor. Pile into a large bowl, pour over the brandy or sherry and mix everything together. Fry the shallots and garlic cloves in the butter until soft-ish and then add to the meats as well as the egg, herbs, breadcrumbs, alcohol, nuts, green peppercorns and juniper berries. Season generously. Press into a small terrine tin of 700 ml / 1 ¼ pint capacity, press down well and cover with foil or a butter paper. Set in a bain-marie and cook for 1 - 1 ½ hours. When cooked, the terrine will have shrunk away from the sides of the tin and clear juices will be visible. Leave to cool, pressing with a light weight to produce a dense and firm terrine.

To serve, slice and hand round with cornichons, Pickled Pears (page 203) or Cumberland Sauce (page 206).

Meat

Buy British and buy locally - the two fundamental essentials! I always get my meat from my trusted butcher who knows the provenance of every beast; how long it has hung for and, importantly, is well qualified in giving top advice on how best to cook every cut. Supermarket meat may well be cheaper but usually lacks flavour and, regrettably, is all too often imported. Neither is there a genie who will jump off the shelves to butcher it according to your wishes.

PANTS-OFF BEEF
(SERVES 6)

For two years I worked for a very swish Swiss Bank in St James's in London. I shared a desk - and plenty of laughs as well - with Di Davison. She was a breath of fresh air with a marvellous turn of phrase. She always swore this receipt had a very successful effect on her boyfriend, hence its name. Indeed, it must have done, as she always breezed into the office with a broad beam the morning after she had dished it up!

- 6 x 150g / 6 oz braising steaks
- Flour for dusting
- 2 tsp Dijon mustard
- 4 tbsp black peppercorns, crushed
- Sea salt
- 2 tbsp olive oil
- 25g / 1 oz butter
- 350g / 12 oz chestnut mushrooms, sliced
- 175ml / 6 fl oz red wine
- 600ml / 1 pint beef stock
- Fresh chives, snipped

Preheat the oven to 170 C. Dust steaks with flour and then spread the mustard on one side. Sprinkle over the crushed peppercorns and season with sea salt.

Heat the oil and butter in a large frying pan until hot. Add the steaks and cook for 2 minutes on each side then transfer to a flameproof casserole and set aside. Add the mushrooms to the frying pan, sautéfor 2 minutes then add the wine. Spoon the mushroom and wine mixture over the steaks, scraping the pan well with a wooden spoon. Add the stock and cover the casserole. Cook in the oven for 1 ½ hours, then remove the lid and cook for a further hour.

To serve, put the steaks into a warmed dish, pour over the sauce and garnish with chives. Potato croquettes and Slow-Roasted Tomatoes (page 122) are excellent accompaniments.

BRAISED OXTAIL
(SERVES 6 - 8)

Good strong beef stock is the key here which, made with the addition of a marrow bone, will produce a marvellous jelly-like consistency. Meltingly tender and mouth-wateringly inviting with its deep rich colour, it is both warming and hefty. I often add prunes half an hour before end cooking time for extra stickiness as well as enriching the gravy. When buying the oxtail look for those which are firm to the touch with dark meaty clusters around the bone - avoid any grey, flabby pieces.

- 1.8 kg / just under 4 lbs oxtail, cut into 3" lengths
- Plain flour
- Tbsp olive oil
- 2 carrots
- 2 sticks celery
- 2 leeks
- 2 onions, peeled and sliced
- 2 glasses red wine
- Juice of an orange
- Bouquet garni
- Bay leaf
- 1 + litre / 2 - 3 pints good beef stock
- Seasoning

Preheat the oven to 170 C. Trim up the oxtail and dust lightly with flour. Heat the olive oil in a large heavy-based casserole and brown the meat thoroughly. You will need to do this in batches then drain on kitchen paper. Trim and quarter the carrots, celery and leeks and add to the pan together with the onions. Cook in the pan for a few minutes then remove from the casserole (stand in a dish on the side). Mix a further tbsp of flour into the casserole with the red wine and bring to the boil, stirring well. Return all the ingredients to the pan and add the orange juice, bouquet garni, bay leaf and pour over sufficient stock to cover then season thoroughly. Bring gently to simmering point on top of the stove, cover and place in the oven for an hour, turning the meat from time to time. Lower the temperature to 140 C and cook for a further 3 hours or until the meat is literally falling off the bone. Cool overnight then discard the fat. Reheat thoroughly in a low oven for 45 minutes until the meat is very hot and the liquid is bubbling at the edges. Remove all the ingredients from the pan then reduce the gravy to required consistency and check the seasoning. Return the contents to the pan and serve with creamy Mashed Potatoes (page 123) or good old-fashioned dumplings.

OX CHEEKS IN PORT AND BALSAMIC

One for the hardcore carnivores. Many of our most flavoursome and interesting cuts of beef end up not on the butcher's counter but in his mincing machine. These are invariably the cheaper cuts but with imagination and careful cooking, they can and do provide excellent eating. The secret is to cook them slowly, taking advantage of their bones, sinew, fat and gelatinous tissue which keeps them juicy and renders them tender. Cooking times are slow but preparation time is brief - another plus for the busy cook.

This receipt comes from Lambourne's Butchers in Stow-on-the-Wold where the quality meat, game and poultry is always of the highest quality, locally sourced and well hung.

- 2 ox cheeks, cleaned
- Olive oil
- 150ml / ¼ pint port
- 150ml / ¼ pint balsamic vinegar
- Red onion, peeled and sliced
- Seasoning
- Tbsp plain flour

Preheat the oven to 160 C. Season the ox cheeks with salt and pepper and rub with a little of the olive oil. Heat a frying pan with no oil and seal the ox cheeks all over. Meanwhile, in a small saucepan, heat together the port and balsamic vinegar then pour into an ovenproof casserole dish and add the onion and the ox cheeks. Place in the oven for 3 ½ hours. When done, remove the ox cheeks from the casserole and thicken the cooking juices with the flour.

Tips FROM THE SINK

- You can also cook lamb shanks in this way, replacing the balsamic vinegar with ¼ pint of stock instead.

BLADE OF BEEF
(SERVES 6 - 8)

I must have dined with the Storeys at least twice a week. Talk about the old proverb 'more hot dinners …' Until I moved from The Red House, they were my closest neighbours and the kindest of friends who happily and generously fed me. Both cook superbly well and now that Mike has retired, he is very likely to be in the kitchen where there is always frenzied activity as he experiments with new ideas including this meltingly flavoursome and punchy dish.

You need to start thinking about this well ahead of time - say on Tuesday for the perfect Friday night dinner to kick-start the weekend. Ask your butcher to prepare a rolled piece of blade of beef.

- 2 ½ kg / 5 lbs + blade of beef
- Olive oil
- Seasoning

Marinade:

- 500ml / 17 fl oz red wine
- 750ml / 1 ¼ pints beef stock
- Onion, roughly chopped
- 2 carrots, chopped
- 3 bay leaves
- Garlic head, sliced crossways
- Bunch thyme
- 2 sprigs rosemary
- Pinches of dry oregano and cracked pepper

Mix all the marinade ingredients together and steep the beef in this for 1 - 2 days in the fridge.

Preheat the oven to 150 C. Take the dish out of the fridge a couple of hours before cooking to allow it to come to room temperature. Remove the meat from the marinade, reserving the liquid, and pat the beef dry. Heat the olive oil in a large casserole and sear the beef until browned all over. Add the reserved marinade, cover with a lid and bring to the boil. Put into the oven for 6 / 7 hours turning halfway through. Take the beef from the casserole and leave to rest covered for 30 minutes. Pass the cooking liquid through a sieve pushing all the goodness from the vegetables. Return to a high heat and reduce by two thirds. Add a knob of butter to give a good glaze to the sauce. Check seasoning. Serve the beef thickly sliced with creamy Mashed Potato (page 123) or Celeriac Dauphinoise (page 121) and hand round the reduced sauce.

CRISP BELLY OF PORK WITH PICKLED PRUNES
(SERVES 6)

Pork:

- 1 ½ kg / 3 lbs pork belly, scored
- Tbsp fennel seeds
- Tbsp coriander seeds
- Tbsp flaked sea salt
- Sunflower oil
- Seasoning
- 600ml / 1 pint dry white wine

Pickled Prunes:

- 500g / 1 lb pitted prunes
- 250ml / 9 fl oz white wine vinegar
- 300g / 10 oz caster sugar
- Cinnamon stick
- 8 juniper berries, crushed
- 8 peppercorns

Cucumber:

- Medium cucumber
- Sea salt
- Tbsp white wine vinegar
- 50g / 2 oz caster sugar
- Tbsp fresh dill leaves, chopped
- Ground white pepper

Prepare the prunes ahead a day or so before. Heat the vinegar, sugar and spices, stirring to melt the sugar then boil until the liquid has reduced by one third and is quite syrupy. Put the prunes into a clean preserving or Kilner jar and pour over the syrup. Cover and leave to stand.

Peel and very thinly slice the cucumber so that they are paper-thin. Layer in a colander with the sea salt and weight to help extract the juices. Leave for a minimum of an hour then blot the slices dry on kitchen paper and mix with the remaining ingredients and set aside.

For the pork, preheat the oven to 220 C. Crush the spices with half the sea salt using a pestle and mortar. Add a couple of tablespoons of oil and rub all over the meat. Rub the skin with more oil and season all over pressing the salt well into the skin to make the crackling crispy. Place in a roasting tray and put in the oven for 30 minutes then pour in half the white wine (around, as opposed to over the skin) and reduce the heat to 170 C cooking for another 1 ½ hours. Add the remainder of the wine half an hour before the end of this cooking time.

Remove the pork from the oven, cover with foil and leave in a warm place to rest for approximately half an hour. Carve and serve with the cooking juices, the prunes and cucumber, hot new potatoes and sour cream.

SAUSAGES WITH LENTILS

Sheer comfort food which almost wraps its arms around you.

- 2 tbsp olive oil
- 8 good quality pork sausages, preferably made by your local butcher
- 2 onions, peeled and sliced
- 100g / 4 oz pancetta, cubed or bacon lardons
- Red chilli, finely chopped, seeded if you like less heat
- 250g / 8 oz Puy lentils
- 150ml / 5 fl oz dry white wine
- 450ml / 16 fl oz light chicken stock
- Seasoning
- Few shakes best balsamic vinegar

Heat the oil in a sauté or frying pan and briefly colour the sausages all over then remove and set aside (they do not need to be cooked through at this stage). Sauté the onions in the same pan until soft but not coloured. Add the pancetta and chopped chilli increasing the heat to give the bacon a good colour and slightly singe the tips of the onions. Add the lentils, wine and stock. Bring to the boil, season, and turn down to a simmer then return the sausages to the pan and season well. Cook for approximately 30 minutes, uncovered, over a gentle heat. The wine and stock will be absorbed as the lentils cook but add a little more liquid if it becomes dry.

To serve, reheat and when hot, add a few shakes of balsamic vinegar to the pan and mix in. Hand round with Salsa Verde (page 218).

LAMBOURNE'S LAZY LAMB WITH REDCURRANT, ORANGE AND WILD GARLIC SAUCE

(SERVES 6)

I use neck fillets for this receipt from new season Cotswold lamb as they are far cheaper than loin fillets – but both work equally well. If using neck fillets just make sure that you trim away the excess fat before cooking.

If you go down to the woods in May, you will find wild garlic growing in profusion. Farmers' markets also sell it and so do glamorous food emporiums such as Fortnum & Mason and Daylesford Farm Shops. When the season has passed, you can always replace this with some fresh mint or sorrel leaves. Similarly, when the redcurrants appear, strip them from their stems and add these.

- 2 lamb fillets
- Tbsp olive oil
- 2 tbsp redcurrant jelly
- Zest and juice of an orange
- Splash of red wine (optional)
- Squirt of runny honey
- Handful of wild garlic leaves, finely shredded
- Seasoning

Preheat the oven to 180 C. Season the trimmed fillets and heat the oil in a baking tin or similar. When hot, seal the lamb all over very briefly until nicely browned – this takes a couple of minutes max. Spread over one tablespoon of the jelly and cook in the oven for 15 minutes. Remove from the heat, transfer to a warmed plate and cover to keep warm. Return the meat pan to the heat, stir in the remaining redcurrant jelly, orange zest and juice and boil up to reduce slightly. Next, add the honey and red wine if using followed by the wild garlic leaves. Season to taste and adjust as necessary.

To serve, carve the meat into thick-ish slices on the diagonal and pour over a little of the sauce then hand the rest around in a jug. Baby spring veggies are delicious with this.

BEST SHEPHERD'S PIE

(SERVES 6 - 8)

A lovingly cooked Shepherd's Pie is the essence of the best comfort food which, simple though it is, never fails to makes the diner feel cherished and cared for. I always start this well ahead. Long, slow cooking is the secret here and the gravy browning and Bovril render it a wonderfully deep colour and enhance its richness of flavour. This receipt uses raw meat but can also be made from a slow-braised shoulder or cooked leg of lamb - in which case reduce the actual cooking time once flavourings and other ingredients have been added to the mince.

- 2 onions
- Tbsp olive oil
- 1.5kg / 3 lbs lamb, minced
- Bay leaf or bouquet garni
- 400g / 10 oz tin of tomatoes
- Good squirt tomato purée
- Tbsp soft brown sugar
- Generous quantity of Worcester sauce
- Tbsp anchovy essence
- Glass red wine
- 225ml / ⅓ pint stock or, if you have any to hand, gravy
- Tbsp gravy browning
- Tbsp Bovril
- Seasoning

- 6 - 7 Maris Piper potatoes
- Milk
- Butter
- Seasoning

Preheat the oven to 140 - 150 C. Peel and slice the onions then heat the oil in a large casserole dish and cook these off gently until softened. Add the mince followed by all the other ingredients, stir well and heat through until there is just a gentle put-put of the liquid. Line the inside of the casserole lid with tinfoil, pop on top and transfer to the oven and cook slowly for at least 4 - 5 hours. I often then move it to the bottom of my two-door Aga and leave it overnight, adding a little more liquid - wine, stock or gravy - if necessary. When thoroughly cooked and a pleasing dark brown, remove the mince from the oven, discard the bay leaf or bouquet garni and leave to cool before refrigerating.

The fat will then solidify on the top and can be removed with a slotted spoon and discarded. Transfer the meat to an ovenproof dish and once again chill.

Peel and boil the potatoes in the usual way, then mash thoroughly making sure it is fairly loose so that it spreads easily. Cover the meat with it and use a fork to make swirly patterns.

Cook in the oven at 190 C for a good 25 minutes until golden brown and bubbling.

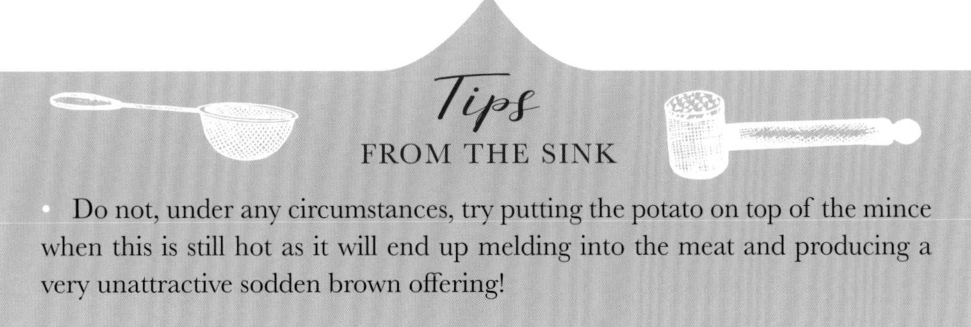

Tips FROM THE SINK

- Do not, under any circumstances, try putting the potato on top of the mince when this is still hot as it will end up melding into the meat and producing a very unattractive sodden brown offering!

Meat

MOROCCAN LAMB
(SERVES 6)

The great thing about stews, casseroles and tagines is that they positively benefit from long, slow cooking and then improve with reheating so you can do this one completely ahead of schedule. It also works incredibly well with a cheaper cut of meat too – shanks, neck fillet/middle neck or shoulder are all fine. I keep the fruit out of the tagine here and usually put it in the couscous served alongside but, if you like, some dried apricots, figs or dates would all go wonderfully well.

- 1 ½ - 2 kgs / 3 ½ - 4 lbs lamb (see above), cubed unless using shanks
- 4 tbsp olive oil
- 8 garlic cloves, crushed
- 4 onions, peeled and sliced
- Tbsp root ginger, peeled and grated
- 1 ½ tsp coriander seeds, crushed
- 3 tsp ground cinnamon
- Cinnamon stick
- Salt & pepper
- Good squirt tomato purée
- 400g tinned tomatoes
- 2 - 3 strips of orange zest
- Aubergine or butternut squash, diced
- 4 - 5 tbsp honey
- Handful each mint and coriander leaves, chopped

Preheat the oven to 150 C. Heat half the oil in a casserole pan and when hot, sear the meat in batches for a few minutes on both sides until nicely coloured. Remove and set aside. Add the rest of the oil to the pan and cook the garlic, onions, ginger and spices until the onions are soft. Season generously with salt and pepper then add the lamb, tomato purée, tomatoes, orange zest, veggies and honey and cover and cook for at least 1 ½ hours in the oven.

To serve, bring to the table in the casserole dish and scatter over the herbs. A bowl of steamed couscous is the obvious pairing here.

OLD FAITHFUL'S CARNE PIZZAIOLA

A dish derived from the Neapolitan tradition which features meat - in this instance veal - cooked with tomatoes, garlic, white wine and other seasonings long enough to tenderise the meat. Old Faithful, who introduced me to this, might not have been the tidiest chef in the kitchen but it was well worth washing up the pots and pans used in order to let him cook on this occasion.

- 4 veal escalopes
- Plain flour
- Seasoning
- Olive oil
- 8 garlic cloves, peeled
- 4 tbsp tomato purée
- Small jar capers, drained
- ½ cup cold water
- Glass white wine
- Tbsp oregano leaves, finely chopped, plus a few extra sprigs to serve
- 300g / 10 oz cherry tomatoes, halved

Place one escalope between two sheets of parchment paper and, using a rolling pin, beat out to flatten. Do the same with the remaining three then season and flour each one. Heat the olive oil in a large, deep frying-pan and brown the cloves of garlic. Once coloured, remove and discard then cook the escalopes, adding more oil if necessary, until just coloured on both sides. Lift from the pan and transfer to a preheated dish and keep warm in the oven.

Squirt the tomato purée into the frying pan and add the capers, white wine, oregano and tomatoes and cook until the tomatoes have broken down and are soft and the sauce is pulpy. Check seasoning then return the escalopes to the pan for a couple of minutes before spooning everything into a warmed dish. Decorate with a few sprigs of oregano and serve.

SLOW-COOKED SHOULDER OF LAMB WITH BEANS

(SERVES 6)

- 4 tbsp olive oil, plus a little extra to finish
- 4 - 5 garlic cloves, chopped
- Tsp fresh thyme leaves
- Sea salt and freshly ground black pepper
- 1.5 kg / 3 - 3 ½ lbs shoulder of lamb, boned and rolled
- 2 carrots, roughly chopped
- Onion, peeled and chopped
- Leek, chopped
- Heaped tbsp tomato purée
- 125ml / ¼ pint red wine
- 1 litre / 2.2 pints good chicken stock
- Tin flageolet beans
- Handful flat-leaf parsley, chopped

Salsa Verde (page 218)

Mix 2 tbsp olive oil with the garlic, thyme and seasoning and rub all over the lamb. Leave to marinate overnight in the fridge. The next day, preheat the oven to 160 C. Heat the rest of the oil in a casserole (one which has a lid) and put in the lamb, brown on all sides, then lift out and put to one side. Add carrots, onion and leek and cook over a low heat for 5 minutes until all are softened but not coloured. Add the tomato purée and red wine and bubble to reduce the liquid by half. Return the lamb to the pot, add stock and pour in enough water to cover the meat. Bring to a simmer, cover and put into the preheated oven for 3 hours, until the lamb is very tender.

Drain the tinned beans into a sieve and rinse through well with cold water to remove the brine then pat dry. Heat the beans through in a pan with a little butter or oil and, if you like, stir in some flat-leaf parsley and spinach leaves to wilt.

Pile the beans into a bowl, hack the lamb up - it should fall to bits - and drizzle over a little olive oil. Hand round the Salsa Verde (page 218).

Tips FROM THE SINK

- Make or buy ready-made salsa verde and stir in a few tablespoons of mayonnaise to make a creamy sauce.

Vegetable Sides

So often, the very mention of the word vegetables conjures up images of them as the ubiquitous pairing 'meat and two veg' whereby they always play the role of bridesmaid. And yet, their best qualities so often surface when they can put on a solo performance. The golden rule which guarantees they are savoured at their finest is to serve them on a seasonal basis.

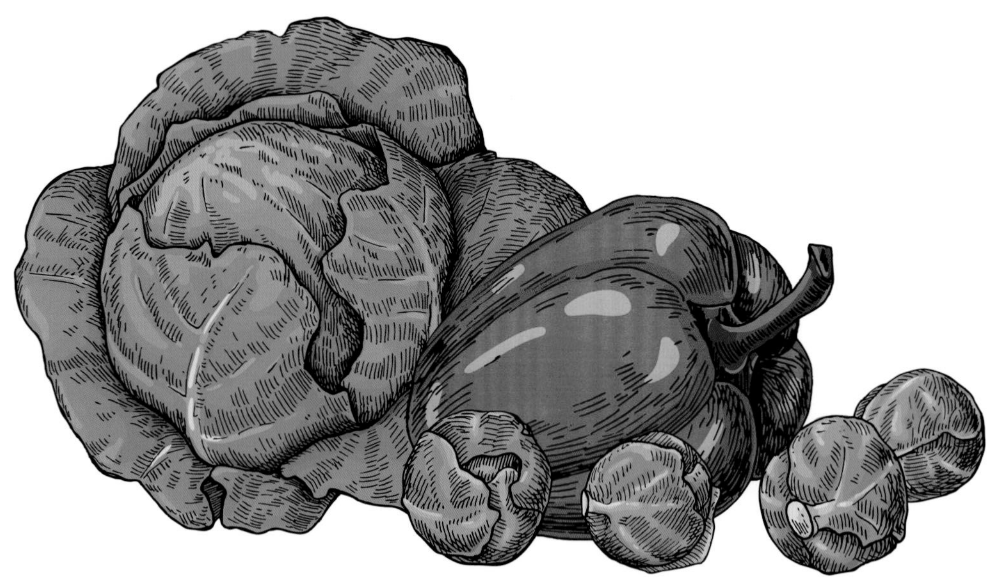

RED HOUSE CARROTS

The great joy of these is that they can be prepared and, if you wish, cooked in advance then reheated.

- Bunch new carrots, topped and tailed, scraped or peeled, halved lengthways
- 50g / 2 oz butter
- Tbsp soft brown sugar
- 2 – 3 star anise
- Fresh tarragon stalks, if to hand
- ½ glass white wine, topped up with water
- Sea salt

Preheat the oven to 180 – 190 C. Arrange the carrots in a smallish roasting tray in a single layer so that they fit snugly. Dot over the butter, sprinkle on the sugar, star anise and fresh tarragon stalks if using. Pour in the white wine and water, scatter with salt and cover with aluminium foil. Bake in the oven for 50 minutes or until just soft when pierced with a knife.

HASSELBACK POTATOES

- 3 - 4 new potatoes per person
- 50g / 2oz butter, softened
- Olive oil
- Sea salt

Preheat the oven to 200 C. Cut a slice off the base of each potato so that it lies flat. With a sharp knife, make a series of cuts vertically without going right through, so that it resembles a crown. Place the potatoes in a well buttered dish or baking tray, smear a little butter over each then season with the salt. Cook as for roast potatoes for approx 45 minutes to an hour, until you have perfect golden potatoes.

HEN'S KALE

Best left until after a flash of mellowing frost before picking, the curly edged plumes of kale have become a winter staple. Try them with toasted macadamia nuts, chorizo or serve as Henrietta Cheetham brings hers to the table so that it resembles an earthy flavoured seaweed.

- 1.2 kg / 2 lbs kale, finely shredded
- Olive oil
- Cayenne pepper
- Sea salt

Preheat the oven to 200 C. Arrange the kale in a large baking tray, pour olive oil all over it then sprinkle with cayenne pepper and sea salt. Toss well and cook for 10 minutes or so, moving the leaves around the pan once or twice until just browned at the edges and crispy.

STIR-FRY BRUSSEL SPROUTS

I always loathed brussel sprouts until I discovered how good they are when prepared thus. Gone is that dreadful memory and stench whilst cooking them akin to bad drains and instead, these have a wonderful nutty flavour with a bit of bite. Remove the bases and outer leaves from sprouts then slice finely – I do this in the Magimix using the slicing blade in a matter of seconds.

- 250g / 8 oz pancetta, cubed or bacon lardons
- Dash olive oil
- 500g / 1 lb brussel sprouts, finely sliced or shredded
- 3 - 4 tbsp toasted sesame oil
- Seasoning

Heat the olive oil in a large frying pan and toss in the pancetta or bacon lardons and cook until nicely browned and crisp. Using a slotted spoon remove these, drain on kitchen paper and set aside. Add the shredded sprouts to the pan plus a little of the sesame oil. Stir constantly for 4 – 5 minutes, adding more sesame oil as required, by which time they should be tinged a golden brown. Remove and transfer to a preheated dish mixing in the lardons, then cover with cling film or foil. I leave these sitting in the warming oven of the Aga quite happily for up to an hour before serving.

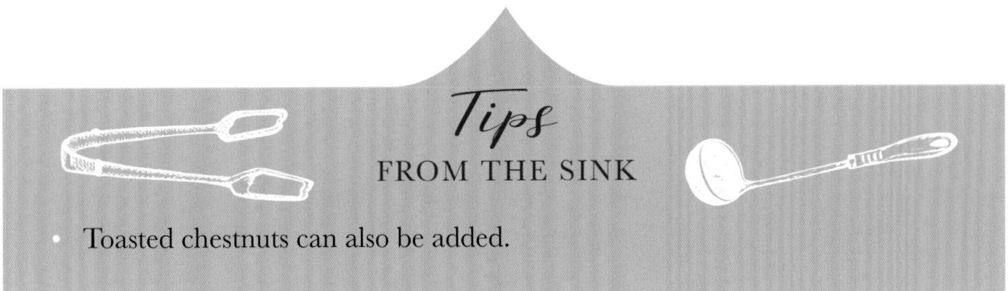

Tips FROM THE SINK

- Toasted chestnuts can also be added.

GIN'S BAKED FENNEL

Ginny Elliot will forever be remembered as one of this country's top equestrian three day event riders and a multi-medal winner, be they for World and European Championships as well as Olympic Gold. Her Sunday lunches are definitely worthy of another. This is one of her specialities and is especially delicious with roast lamb.

- 4 fennel bulbs
- 2 tbsp olive oil
- Seasoning
- 300 ml / ½ pint double cream
- 100g / 4 oz Parmesan, grated
- Cherry tomatoes on the vine

Preheat the oven to 180 C. Trim and thinly slice the fennel bulbs then sauté in the olive oil until soft. Turn into an ovenproof dish and season. Pour over the double cream and grated Parmesan then top with the tomatoes and bake for approx 20 minutes until golden brown and bubbling.

ROASTED FENNEL

(SERVES 8)

An alternative version, this time without cream.

- 4 fennel bulbs
- Dried red chilli, crumbled
- ½ tsp fennel seeds
- Zest and juice of ½ lemon
- Splash of dry white wine or dry sherry
- 60ml / 2 fl oz olive oil
- Sea salt and freshly ground pepper

Preheat the oven to 200 C. Remove the tough outer layers from the fennel bulbs and cut each one into quarters lengthwise. Place the fennel in a bowl and crumble over the chilli, season and toss through the fennel seeds. Squeeze over the lemon juice and anoint with the olive oil. Toss well to combine then tip into a baking tray, cover with foil and roast for 30 minutes, then remove the foil and continue to cook for a further 15 minutes.

CELERIAC DAUPHINOISE
(SERVES 6)

Whilst the gnarled and knobbly celeriac won't ever win a prize in a beauty contest, it possesses star qualities which belie its looks. This is ideal with game or makes a change from the potato dish of this name.

- 100g / 4 oz dried morel or cep mushrooms
- Large head celeriac or two smaller ones, peeled and thinly sliced
- Lemon juice
- 300 - 450 ml / ½ - ¾ pint double cream
- Celery salt and black pepper

Preheat the oven to 180 - 190 C. Soak the mushrooms in a bowl filled with boiling water to cover for at least 10 - 15 minutes then drain, reserving the liquid. Put this into a saucepan together with the cream and boil to reduce until slightly thicker than the original consistency. Cook the celeriac in boiling salted water to which a little lemon juice has been added. When the slices are soft, drain and pat dry. Fry off the ceps in a pan with a little butter for a few minutes.

Arrange a layer of celeriac to cover the base of an ovenproof dish, seasoning with the celery salt and pepper then dot over the ceps. Repeat the process to fill the dish then pour over the creamy mixture. Bake in the oven for 30 - 35 minutes until the top is nicely browned.

JANSSON'S TEMPTATION
(SERVES 6 - 8)

No winter should pass without serving this Swedish potato dish up for supper. Freshly baked and bubbling, it is the absolute essence of how delicious the modest tuber truly is.

- 1.2 kg / 2 lbs potatoes, peeled and cut into batons
- Seasoning
- 2 onions, peeled and finely chopped
- Tin of anchovy fillets
- 400ml / 14 fl oz whole milk
- 1 litre / 2.2 pints double cream

Preheat the oven to 160 C. Put the potatoes into a bowl, season thoroughly with salt and black pepper then add the onion and anchovies. Turn into an ovenproof dish and pour over the milk and cream. Cover with foil and bake for 30 minutes then remove the foil and continue to cook for at least another 30 minutes until the middle feels soft and the top starts to crisp.

SLOW-ROASTED TOMATOES

Serve with meats or in salads or purée them and add to soups.

- 4 large flavoursome tomatoes, halved
- Pinch of sugar
- Sea salt
- Mixed dried herbs
- Olive oil

Preheat the oven to 120 C. Arrange the tomatoes on a baking tray, cut side up, scatter on the sugar, add a sprinkling of sea salt and dried herbs. Trickle over a little olive oil and roast in the oven for 3 - 4 hours until semi-dried.

MASHED POTATO

The humble tuber is one of the treasures of the earth. Quite literally. It presents the cook with limitless ways in which it may be served. Who can resist properly roasted potatoes - crunchy on the exterior and with fluffy insides; the first new potatoes of the season the size of pebbles, sweet tasting and buttery in their own right; a plateful of pommes frites; a dreamy-creamy dauphinoise; steaming baked potatoes with crispy skins; pommes parmentier; potato patties fried in bacon fat and so many more. I grew up believing that Ireland was the land of the potato and that, quite simply, was that. I have since come to appreciate that the potato is one of the world's best-loved vegetables and everyone has their own personal favourite way of enjoying them. For me, unctuously smooth mashed potato is hard to rival and it makes the perfect bedfellow to so many dishes.

- 4 large floury potatoes - i.e. King Edward's or Maris Piper, peeled and cut into chunks
- 100 ml / 3 ½ fl oz full-fat milk
- 100 ml / 3 ½ fl oz olive oil
- Seasoning

In an ideal world, bake the spuds until tender, then leave to cool before halving and scooping out the flesh and mashing until lump-free. This takes time though so the usual method is to boil the potatoes in salted water until they are soft. Do not go on cooking them until they have become a mush, otherwise they will have absorbed too much water and the end result will resemble smash. If boiling, drain well and return to the saucepan, cover with a tea towel and leave them to dry out for 5 minutes. Bring the milk and olive oil to the boil in a small pan. Meanwhile, mash the potatoes very thoroughly then pass the mixture through a potato ricer or sieve for extra smoothness. Beat in the milk and olive oil and season well with salt and freshly ground white pepper.

OVEN-ROASTED VEGETABLES
(SERVES 6)

When I lived in London, Janie Tate and I gave an annual lunch party on the Sunday before Christmas. The menu never changed - hot baked ham, cheese-filled jacket potatoes and Janie's vegetables as below. Despite its obvious simplicity, guests never seemed to want to go home; not least the current writer of The Spectator magazine's Drink Column. How well I recall leaving this larger-than-life journalist; his love of food ably matched, quite naturally, by that of his passion for claret, still lolling on the sofa - a well replenished glass in hand - as I headed out to dinner much later on. I'm not sure he was much help with the washing up either.

- 450g / 14 oz cherry tomatoes
- 2 medium courgettes, diagonally sliced
- Small aubergine, ends discarded and cut into rounds
- Red and yellow pepper, seeded and cut into strips
- 2 garlic cloves, peeled and finely chopped
- 2 red onions, peeled and chopped
- Handful fresh basil leaves
- 4 tbsp olive oil
- Parmesan shavings

Preheat the oven to 200 C. Arrange all the vegetables in a large roasting tin, and scatter the garlic over them. Tear up the basil leaves and mix with the olive oil then pour over. Bake until just soft (approx 35 - 40 minutes). When ready, cover with shavings of Parmesan.

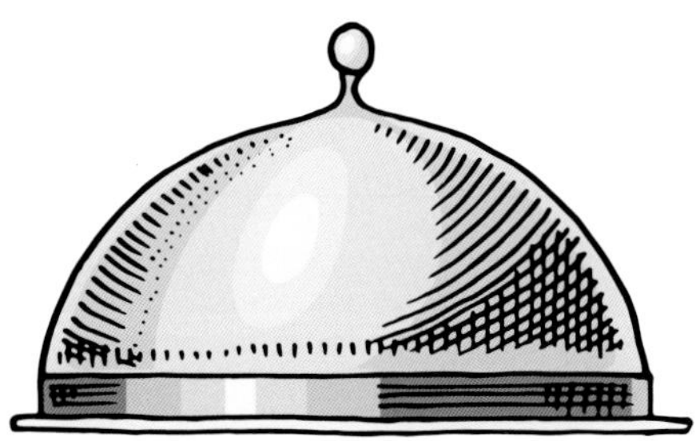

COURGETTE FRITTERS

In 2010, I had the honour of being invited to participate in HRH The Prince of Wales's 'Garden Party with a Difference' held at Clarence House which concentrated on organic, seasonal hero foods. I can remember the occasion vividly as just hours before I was at Goresbridge Horse Sales in Ireland - in the middle of nowhere - with a friend who was negotiating to buy a horse. Didn't this animal just have to be the final Lot in the catalogue? Panic was beginning to rise and my fists went clammy at the thought of being a 'no-show'. Luckily, I caught the last flight home that night by the skin of my teeth knowing I had to be in the Royal Cookery Theatre first thing the following morning. Here is one of the dishes I demonstrated which was served with a cobnut salad - all suitably seasonal.

- 500g / 1 lb medium courgettes
- 2 tbsp herbs - i.e. basil, marjoram, flat-leaf parsley, chopped
- 3 spring onions, white part only, finely chopped
- 3 eggs, beaten
- Heaped tbsp plain flour
- Zest of a lemon
- Freshly ground white pepper
- Olive oil

- Lettuce leaves, preferably inner ones from a buttery home-grown floppy lettuce or assortment
- Handful cobnuts, shelled
- Hazelnut or walnut oil
- Seasoning

Grate the courgettes and salt them, then turn into a colander and leave them to drain. Using a clean tea towel, wring out the excess water from the courgettes and put into a large mixing bowl together with the herbs, spring onions, eggs, flour and lemon zest and season with freshly ground white pepper. Next, heat approx 2 tbsp olive oil in a large heavy-based pan and when hot, drop tablespoons of the mixture into the pan and, using the back of a spoon flatten them out slightly. Cook for 2 - 3 minutes and, when the bottom is golden brown and crisp, then flip over and repeat cooking process. When ready, remove and pat dry on kitchen paper.

To serve, arrange each patty on some leaves which have been anointed with the hazelnut or walnut oil and seasoned, then scatter over the toasted cobnuts.

STUFFED MUSHROOMS
(SERVES 2)

A favourite Sunday night supper dish when the egg basket is empty. The variations as to what to fill these with are limitless. It all depends what is in the fridge or vegetable rack.

- Nut of butter
- Tbsp olive oil
- 4 large flat mushrooms, peeled and stalks removed
- Tot of sherry
- Squeeze lemon juice
- Garlic clove, peeled and crushed
- 250g / 8 oz spinach/chard leaves, wilted until soft then thoroughly drained
- 4 rashers streaky bacon, cooked until crisp and crumbled, or 2 slices smoked ham, diced
- 75g / 3 oz blue cheese - i.e. Stilton, crumbled
- Seasoning
- 2 tbsp breadcrumbs

Preheat the oven to 180 C. Heat the butter and oil in a large frying pan, add the mushrooms, tot of sherry and lemon juice and cook gently on both sides until soft and floppy. Remove and set aside then scrape in the garlic and cook for 2 - 3 minutes before scooping out and mixing in with the spinach. Arrange the mushrooms in an ovenproof dish. Divide the spinach between them, dot over the bacon (or ham) and crumble over the cheese. Sprinkle on the breadcrumbs and cook in the oven for 10 - 15 minutes until bubbling. Serve immediately.

NELLA'S BROAD BEANS

- 350g / 10 oz broad beans
- Béchamel sauce (page 212)
- 3 tbsp flat-leaf parsley leaves, finely chopped

Cook the broad beans and drain. If you can be bothered, and it really is worth the effort, shell the outer skins and discard these. Mix the beans in to the béchamel sauce which has been heated through. Stir in the parsley and transfer to an ovenproof dish.

To serve, place in a moderate oven and heat through, approximately 15 minutes.

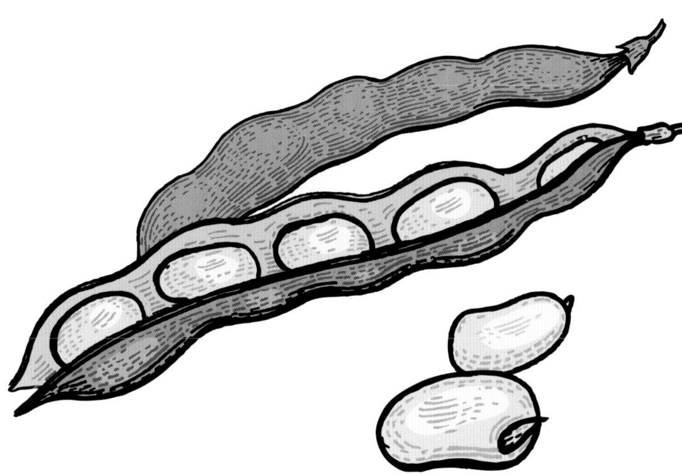

Puddings

For so many of us, nostalgia about puddings is associated with happy childhood memories; the sort one's mother and indeed her mother would serve. Some classics have rightly remained totally unchanged whilst others have been given a novel twist to modernise them. Whatever your preference, puddings are for pure pleasure rather than for sin - so banish those feelings of guilt and weak protestations of 'I really shouldn't' - indulge and just enjoy them!

BASIL AND LIME PANNA COTTA
(SERVES 6)

- 600 ml / 1 pint double cream
- 75g / 3 oz caster sugar
- Zest of two limes
- Tbsp torn basil leaves, plus tbsp thinly shredded basil leaves
- Juice of one lime
- 1 ½ - 2 gelatine leaves

Put the gelatine leaves into a bowl filled with ice cold water and stand to one side for 10 - 12 minutes until soft and floppy. Meanwhile, gently heat the cream and sugar in a heavy-based pan and allow the sugar to dissolve. When the cream boils, remove from the heat and add the lime zest and the first tablespoon of torn basil leaves. Leave to infuse for 30 minutes then strain. Return the liquid to a pan and warm through. Add the squeezed out gelatine leaves and the thinly shredded basil plus the lime juice, mixing well. Pour into individual moulds or small glasses and leave to set.

Serve with lime wedges and basil plus some biscuits - i.e. Penny's Chocolate Biscuits (page 165).

GREEN GODDESS FRUIT SALAD

Gone are the days of the traditional 'fruit salad' - a truly dispiriting affair invariably involving several tinned varieties and garnished with glacé cherries (a dated look if ever there was one). How times have changed. By contrast, my lifelong friend Susie Wilson's mélange dances with decadence. The inclusion of the avocado may surprise but it works extremely well.

- 2 green apples
- 2 pears
- Tin lychees, stoned
- 2 kiwi
- Avocado, ripe
- Pink grapefruit

Syrup:

- 200ml / 7 fl oz sugar syrup (page 225)
- 150ml / ¼ pint pink grapefruit juice
- Squeeze of lime

Add the grapefruit juice and lime to the sugar syrup over a gentle heat then leave to cool.

Quarter the apples, core and, leaving their skins on, chop into pieces squeezing over some lemon juice to prevent discolouring. Peel the pears, core and cut up similarly and put into a pretty bowl. Drain the lychees, peel and slice the kiwis, avocado and pink grapefruit and add these, mixing in gently. Pour on the sugar syrup. Serve with Hazelnut Shortbread (page 164).

PINEAPPLE AND MINT

This is sheer simplicity and comes from Liz Bowden who is a strong advocate of all things menthol - bar those filthy flavoured fags!

- Pineapple, ripe
- 600 ml / 1 pint water
- 250g / 8 oz granulated sugar
- Generous handful fresh mint leaves, very finely chopped

Cut the skin off the pineapple and slice into rings. Chop each one into triangular shapes, discarding the central core, and toss the pieces into a glass bowl. Put the water and sugar into a saucepan and boil hard to make a syrup then pour into a jug and leave to cool. Just before serving, pour the syrup over the fruit and stir in the mint.

STRAWBERRIES IN COINTREAU

- 2 punnets ripe, flavoursome strawberries
- Zest and juice of two oranges
- 2 tbsp icing sugar
- Cointreau, to taste

Simply slice or halve the strawberries and mix gently with the orange zest and juice. Sprinkle on the icing sugar and add Cointreau – how much will depend on how boozy you like your puddings – and leave to stand for at least an hour before serving.

CITRUS COMPOTE WITH ROSEMARY

(SERVES 6)

This looks beautiful and makes a refreshing winter pudding. Experiment with other flavourings such as mint or star anise instead of the rosemary.

- 275ml / 9 ¾ fl oz freshly squeezed orange juice (bought is fine)
- 175ml / 6 fl oz water
- 150g / 6 oz caster sugar
- 3 sprigs fresh rosemary
- Juice of ½ lemon
- 2 oranges
- 3 blood oranges
- Yellow grapefruit
- Ruby grapefruit

Heat the orange juice with the water, sugar and one sprig of rosemary, stirring from time to time to help the sugar dissolve. Once it has, bring to the boil then simmer for approximately 20 minutes until the mixture is slightly syrupy. You should have about 300ml /10 fl oz of liquid by this stage. Remove from the heat, add the lemon juice and the remaining two rosemary sprigs.

Segment the oranges and grapefruits - it's a bit of a fiddle but the best way of ensuring there is no pith or membrane. Put these into a shallow bowl or dish, preferably glass, and pour over the syrup. Serve with either Tunisian Citrus Cake (page 141) or with the Hazelnut Shortbread (page 179)

STRAWBERRY, ALMOND AND LEMON TART
(SERVES 8)

The strawberry is all part and parcel of an English summer - be it for Ascot, Wimbledon, Glyndebourne, picnics, indulgent cream teas or simply for eating straight from the straw-laden fruit beds. Ripe, flavoursome berries, however, are all. And scent too. A strawberry that is going to taste good must smell good. This is best assembled just before you want to eat it but you can have everything ready beforehand.

- 320g / 10 oz packet ready-rolled sweet shortcrust pastry
- Egg white

- 450g / just under 1 lb mascarpone
- 225g / 9 oz fromage frais
- Grated zest and juice of 2 lemons
- Few drops almond essence
- 10 tbsp icing sugar, sieved
- 750g / 1 ½ lbs ripe and ready strawberries, hulled

Preheat the oven to 200 C. Dust a worktop with icing sugar and roll out the pastry and line a 23cm / 9" tart tin with a removable base. Prick all over with a fork and put in the fridge for 30 minutes. Bake blind for approximately 12 minutes then remove the paper and beans and brush with the egg white and return to the oven for a further 6 - 7 minutes until pale gold. Leave to cool in the tin and then remove the pastry case and place on a flat platter.

Beat the mascarpone with a wooden spoon until it is quite soft then add the fromage frais, lemon zest and juice, almond essence and icing sugar.

Just before serving, spread this mixture inside the pastry shell and cover with the strawberries making sure you cram in as many as possible to cover up the filling. Dust with a little more icing sugar and bring to the table.

TREACLE TART
(SERVES 6 - 8)

With its creamy lemon custard filling this is less cloying than the classic tart and less likely to pull out your teeth. Similarly, the inclusion of the orange zest injects extra 'lift' to the end result.

- 320g / 10 oz ready-rolled sweet shortcrust pastry
- 2 eggs, lightly beaten
- 150ml / ¼ pint sour cream
- 100g / 4 oz fine white breadcrumbs
- 350g / 12 oz golden syrup
- Zest and juice of a lemon
- Grated zest of an orange
- 3 tbsp ground almonds

Preheat the oven to 190 C. On a well-floured surface, roll out the pastry and line a 20cm / 9" tin with a removable base. Next, mix the eggs with the sour cream and then add the breadcrumbs, syrup and zest and juice of the lemon and orange zest. Spread the ground almonds over the base of the pastry shell and pour on the mixture. Cook in the oven for approximately 30 - 35 minutes. Best served hot or warm, with thick cream and/or Custard (page 224). This also reheats well.

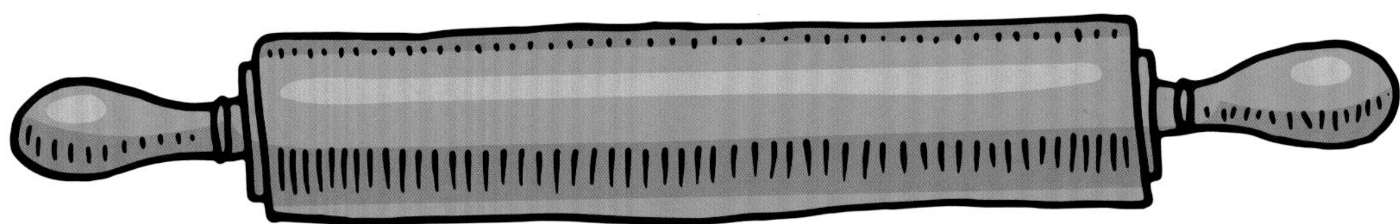

BAKEWELL TART
(SERVES 8)

As a frangipane freak, this one is high on my list. It's also very good at tea instead of the more traditional fruit or sponge cake.

- 500g / 1lb 2 oz sweet shortcrust pastry – I buy ready-made
- 5 tbsp raspberry jam, warmed
- 100g / 4 oz unsalted butter
- 100g / 4 oz caster sugar
- 3 eggs plus 1 egg white
- ½ tsp almond essence
- 150g / 6 oz ground almonds
- Granulated sugar

Preheat the oven to 190 C. Grease a 24cm / 9 ½" tart tin with a loose base. Roll out the pastry to approx 3mm thickness and line the tart tin, pricking the base all over. Place in the fridge for 20 minutes or so and then line with baking paper and fill with baking beans or rice and bake the shell for approx 10 - 15 minutes before removing the beans and paper and brushing the base with egg white. Return to the oven to a further 5 minutes until golden and crisp. Leave to cool before spreading the jam over the base.

Beat the butter and sugar together until pale and fluffy then slowly add the eggs, one at a time, plus the almond essence. Fold in the ground almonds and spoon the mixture into the tart case. Sprinkle with the granulated sugar and cook for approx 45 minutes until lightly coloured on the top. I leave to cool and then remove the tin and transfer to a large plate. Serve with plenty of thick cream.

FARMHOUSE APPLE PIE

Apples - another of nature's wonders which adapt and lend themselves so generously to a limitless number of dishes, both sweet and savoury. This pie, which is reassuringly rustic and simple to make, can be made using whatever variety of apples are to hand though remember, cookers will be less sweet than the cultivated kind and may require additional sugar. Replace the sultanas with brambles when they are in season and omit the cinnamon. Generally accompanied with cream or ice-cream, Yorkshire men will, by tradition, eat theirs with a lump of crumbly cheese, such as Lancashire, Cheshire or Wensleydale. Cheddar is another popular option and is sometimes cooked within the pie.

- 500g / 1 lb apples, peeled, cored and thinly sliced
- 50g / 2 oz caster or Demerara sugar
- Tsp cinnamon
- Zest of a lemon
- Handful sultanas, soaked in boiling water then drained
- 320g / 10 oz shortcrust pastry (there will be some leftover so freeze for another time)
- Milk
- Caster sugar

Preheat the oven to 190 C. Cut the apples into a pie dish and sprinkle over the sugar, cinnamon, lemon zest and sultanas. Roll out ¾ of the pastry slightly larger than the size of the dish and a strip to fit the edge of the dish. Dampen the edge then fit on the pastry strip, pressing it firmly and dampen this also. Drape the large sheet of rolled pastry over the top, knock up and flute the edges. Make a steam hole in the centre.

Brush the surface of the pastry with milk and sprinkle over a light dusting of caster sugar. Put the dish on a baking sheet and cook in the oven for 30 - 35 minutes until golden brown. Check that the fruit is cooked by inserting a skewer. If it still feels firm, return to the oven for a little longer.

Serve with thick cream, vanilla ice-cream or Calvados Cream (page 224).

TRIFLE
(SERVES 8)

Once a landmark of English cooking, there's no escaping the fact that there are some incredibly unpalatable versions of this pudding. When properly made, however, it is a class act and I think it is particularly appropriate when served on celebratory occasions as a change from a cake. It is the marriage of an alcohol-sodden sponge buried in a pool of custard, jam and whipped cream all piled into a large cut-glass bowl which make this so splendid. If you can be bothered, do make the sponge yourself. Alternatively, use amaretti, macaroons or ratafias. Jelly within is a no-no but the inclusion of best quality raspberry jam and bananas are both musts!

- 300ml / ½ pint whipping cream
- 300ml / ½ pint milk
- Vanilla pod, split lengthways
- 4 egg yolks
- 25g / 1 oz caster sugar
- ½ homemade sponge cake or 200g / 12 oz biscuits, as above
- 200ml / 7 fl oz sherry
- 4 tbsp good quality raspberry jam, warmed
- 2 bananas, peeled and sliced
- 300ml / ½ pint double cream, whipped to form soft peaks
- 50g / 2 oz flaked almonds, lightly toasted

Begin by making the custard. In a saucepan, scald the whipping cream and milk with the vanilla pod, whisking briefly to disperse the seeds. Remove the pan from the heat, set to one side and cover, leaving to infuse. Beat the egg yolks with the sugar and strain the vanilla-flavoured cream onto the eggs and mix thoroughly. Return to the cream pan and cook very gently over a low flame until the custard has thickened. Cut the sponge into bite-size pieces and spread with a little raspberry jam and place into a large glass bowl. Add the sliced bananas. Pour over the custard then top with the whipped cream. Decorate with the flaked almonds then cover and chill for 3 hours minimum before serving.

TIRAMISU
(SERVES 6)

There isn't a definitive classic recipe for this Italian dolce but nevertheless, it is a 'stand out' pudding which I find totally irresistible. The combination of strong coffee, coffee liqueur, chocolate and the rich creaminess of the mascarpone make it food heaven in my book.

- 3 egg yolks
- 2 egg whites
- 50g / 2 oz caster sugar
- 250g / 8 oz mascarpone (one tub)
- 250g / 8 oz packet boudoir sponge fingers
- 175ml / 6 fl oz very strong espresso coffee
- 4 tbsp Kahlúa (coffee liqueur) or substitute with Marsala or rum
- 75g / 3 oz dark chocolate, grated
- Cocoa powder, to decorate

Take the mascarpone from the fridge and bring to room temperature, then break it up a bit using a spoon. Whisk the egg yolks together with the sugar very thoroughly until light and frothy then, bit by bit, add the mascarpone and blitz until well combined and smooth. In a separate clean bowl, whip the egg whites until they form soft peaks, then fold these into the cheese mixture.

Pour the coffee and liqueur into a shallow dish and dip one third of the sponge fingers into this briefly, turning them over. They turn soft very quickly so be swift otherwise all will just disintegrate. Arrange a layer in the base of a handsome glass bowl, cover with some of the mascarpone, then add some grated chocolate and repeat the process twice more. Finish off with a dusting of cocoa powder then cover with cling film and chill for several hours and serve directly from the fridge.

FRUIT JUMBLE CRUMBLE

(SERVES 6 - 8)

Comfort food heaven. I use whatever fruits are to hand. In this instance, my mélange includes apples and pears, strawberries and rhubarb but feel free to mix and match.

Crumble:

- 250g / 8 oz cold unsalted butter, cut into small cubes
- 400g / 12 oz plain flour
- 200g / 6 oz golden caster sugar
- Generous pinch of salt
- 2 tbsp golden syrup

Using the tips of your fingers, crumble up the first four ingredients in a large bowl until they resemble very fine, individual crumbs. Set aside until required.

Fruit:

- 6 - 8 sticks of rhubarb, trimmed and cut into 2" pieces
- 3 tbsp soft brown sugar
- 2 apples, peeled, cored and roughly chopped
- 2 pears, peeled, cored and quartered
- 300g / ½ lbs strawberries, hulled
- Tbsp caster sugar
- Juice of ½ lemon
- Few thin flakes butter

Preheat the oven to 180 C. Arrange the rhubarb in a baking dish, sprinkle over the sugar, cover with parchment paper and roast in the oven for 10 - 12 minutes until just soft to the touch. Remove and set aside. Put the remaining fruits into a saucepan, add the sugar, lemon juice and butter, and heat gently just until the fruit begins to break down. Transfer to an ovenproof dish, add the rhubarb then pile the crumble mixture on top. Drizzle over the syrup and cook for approximately 25 minutes until the topping is golden and the juices are bubbling to the surface around the edges.

SUMMER PUDDING STACKS
(SERVES 8)

A summer without Summer Pudding is unthinkable. And yet, floppy white bread just doesn't do it for me - it renders this dessert a dismal disappointment. So, jettison the Mother's Pride and make it using brioche loaf instead. Individual puddings are also easier to serve and look far more elegant. You will need 8 cutters, 5 - 6 cm in diameter.

- 750g / 1 ½ lb blackcurrants (bag of frozen berries is fine)
- Loaf brioche bread, very thinly cut into 16 slices, crusts removed
- 450g / 12 oz strawberries, hulled and sliced crossways
- 450g / 12 oz raspberries
- 150g / 6 oz blueberries or blackberries, halved
- 150g / 6 oz redcurrants, stripped from their stalks
- 75g / 3 oz caster sugar
- Extra fruit and sprigs of mint for decoration

Start by making the blackcurrant coulis. Tip the fruits into a saucepan, add a little water and cook gently until softened to a pulp. Taste and add a little sugar if necessary. Remove from the pan and blitz in the food processor until smooth then pass through a sieve. Pour this into a shallow dish.

Cover a baking sheet or similar with parchment paper, then arrange the circular cutters on the surface.

Put the remaining fruits into a bowl and combine gently. If too tart, sprinkle in some sugar. Using one of the cutters, stamp out 16 rounds from the bread.

Briefly dip a brioche round into the coulis to coat on both sides and then place in the base of the cutter. Spoon in fruit to fill then top with a further fruited round of bread. Press down lightly. Repeat the process to make the other puddings.

To serve, slide a spatula under the cutter and transfer each stack to a plate and lift off the cutter, using a palette knife if necessary. Decorate the top of each one with the extra fruit, a sprig of mint and perhaps a shake of icing sugar and hand round a jug of thick cream plus any remaining coulis.

TUNISIAN CITRUS CAKE
(SERVES 6 - 8)

This delectable citrus-soaked cake manages to be light and fluffy, as well as scrumptiously sticky. If using polenta, as opposed to breadcrumbs, this is also gluten-free.

- 75g / 3 oz polenta or stale breadcrumbs
- 125g / 5 oz ground almonds
- Tsp baking powder
- Zest of an orange, lemon and lime
- 200ml / 7 fl oz sunflower/olive oil mixed
- 175g / 7 oz caster sugar
- 4 eggs, whisked

Syrup:

- Juice of an orange, lemon and lime
- 75g / 3 oz caster sugar
- 2 tbsp Cointreau (optional)
- 4 cardamon pods
- Cinnamon stick
- 2 star anise

Preheat the oven to 160 C. Oil and line the base of a 9" / 22 cm cake tin. Mix all the dry ingredients together in a bowl and add the zest of each fruit. In another bowl, whisk the oils into the eggs and add to the dry mixture. If the mixture is a little stiff, add a little of the juices reserved for the syrup. Turn into the cake tin and bake in the oven for around 40 minutes or until a skewer, when inserted, comes out clean. When ready, remove from the oven and pierce the surface of the cake all over with a skewer to make holes.

In the meantime, prepare the syrup by heating all the ingredients, swirling the pan until the sugar dissolves and bring to the boil then simmer for a few minutes. Remove from the heat and drizzle half over the cooked citrus cake to 'feed' it. Before serving, pour over the remaining syrup then cut into slices.

STICKY GINGERBREAD PUDDING
(SERVES 6-8)

A true winter warmer and undeniably a steaming pile of starch to ward off cold temperatures. Ideally, this is best made in advance and then reheated when it becomes darker, richer and more aromatic. And don't stint, this cries out for Custard (page 224).

- Tin black treacle
- Tin golden syrup
- 125g / 5 oz butter, room temperature
- 150g / 6 oz self-raising flour
- 3 tsp ground ginger
- Tsp each ground cinnamon and allspice
- 3 eggs
- 2 tbsp ginger wine
- 4 nuggets stem ginger, finely diced

Stand the tins of treacle and syrup in a pan of hot water for about 15 minutes - or else leave them on top of the Aga - this makes them runny and hence easier to spoon out. Grease a pudding basin of 2½ - 3 pint capacity plus a circle of greaseproof paper large enough to cover the pudding. Dice the butter and beat until creamy and light. Add 4 level tablespoons each of treacle and syrup and whizz again to mix in well. Beat in the eggs one at a time then sift the flour with the ground spices and blend them into the pudding mixture. Stir in the ginger wine and finally add the stem ginger. Measure a further 3 tablespoons each of the treacle and syrup into the base of the buttered basin and then top with the pudding mixture.

Cover the basin with the buttered paper and then a sheet of tin foil and secure this lid firmly under the basin rim with string. Place in a saucepan of boiling water half way up the sides of the basin and steam for two hours, topping up the pan with extra boiling water as necessary. If the pudding is to be served immediately, run a palette knife around the inside of the basin and turn out onto a hot plate. Alternatively, leave the sponge to cool in the basin, still wrapped, and store in a cold place until required. Reheat it by boiling for a further hour and then unmould as above.

CHOCOLATE ORANGE PUDDING
(SERVES 8)

I first made this having been given one of those large, exotically decorated boxes of panettone for Christmas by the flamboyant Bucci, much loved proprietor of Frantoio Restaurant in London's King's Road. I considered various ways of enjoying it - bar simply opening it up and consuming it as one would a cake, and decided to use it for an upmarket style Bread & Butter pudding. Forget the butter, however! I served it for my annual post Christmas lunch party with slight trepidation but it went down well enough to merit becoming an annual fixture. There are never any leftovers. This benefits from being prepared the day before or, if that isn't possible, then at least a few hours in advance of being cooked.

- 750g / 1 lb 8 oz panettone
- 50g / 2 oz dark chocolate chips
- 750ml / 1 ¼ pints fresh custard/crème pâtissière (for speed, buy readymade cartons)
- 75ml / 3 fl oz milk
- Zest of two oranges
- 3 egg yolks
- 2 tbsp Cointreau
- 2 tbsp Demerara sugar

Preheat the oven to 160 C. Cut the panettone into 1" / 2½ cm rounds and halve the larger slices. Butter a 3 ½ pint ovenproof dish and arrange the bread in this. Scatter over most of the chocolate chips. In a saucepan, heat the custard, milk and orange zest, allow to cool slightly then whisk in the egg yolks and add the Cointreau. Pour over the panettone and leave to soak preferably overnight (covered and refrigerated) or for a minimum of 4 hours. Finish off by strewing the remaining choc chips over the surface and then sprinkle with the Demerara sugar. Cook in the oven for 25 minutes or so until golden brown and slightly risen and serve hot with thick double cream.

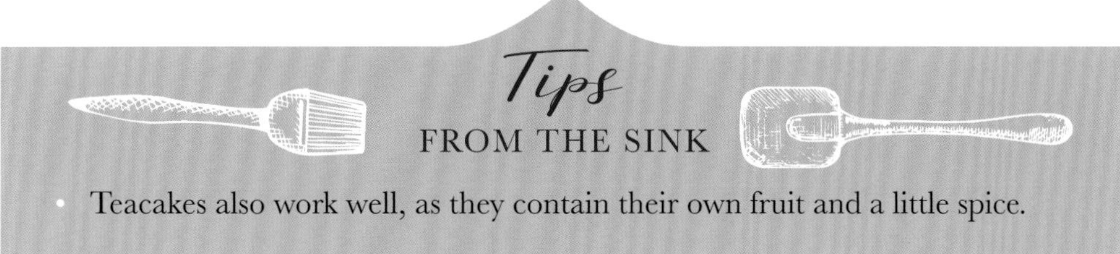

Tips FROM THE SINK

- Teacakes also work well, as they contain their own fruit and a little spice.

CARAMELISED APPLE RICE PUDDING

(SERVES 6)

It took me years to recover from the repertoire of bland milk puddings that were dished up - or perhaps more aptly I should say 'slopped-up' to us at school. All were unfailingly married with stewed apples, scarcely peeled let alone cored, and riddled with pip. Happily reincarnated, this bears no resemblance to such horrors - it is light and creamy and the caramel apples are a pleasing addition.

- Small nut of butter
- 4 tbsp jam, warmed
- 100ml / 3 ½ fl oz water
- 100g / 4 oz caster sugar, plus extra for sprinkling
- 2 green apples, peeled, cored and diced
- 600ml / 1 pint milk
- 200ml / 7 fl oz double cream
- Zest of an orange
- 75g / 3 oz round grain pudding rice
- Tsp ground cinnamon

Preheat the oven to 150 C and lightly butter an ovenproof dish. Spread the jam over the base. Put the water and sugar in a heavy based saucepan and bring to the boil. Continue to boil until the sugar starts to turn to caramel. When it is a rich chestnut brown, carefully drop the apple chunks into the pan. Reduce the heat and stir so that the apples are thoroughly coated with the caramel. Transfer them to the bottom of the dish.

In a bowl, mix the milk, cream, orange zest and rice and add to the dish on top of the apples. Sprinkle the top with half the cinnamon. Place in the oven and bake for 2 hours, stirring the rice layer after the first 30 minutes. After 45 minutes sprinkle over the remaining cinnamon and the sugar.

When ready, the rice should be creamy and swollen, almost mousse-like to the touch, and the top will be golden brown.

SALTED CRÈME CARAMEL
(SERVES 8)

Good old crème caramel has always been something of a national institution parked up, on the pudding trolley, along with the trifle and meringues made to look like swans. Here, however, it is taken to a new level.

- 700ml / 1¼ pints milk
- Vanilla pod
- 5 eggs
- 75g / 3 oz caster sugar

Caramel:

- 125g / 5 oz white caster sugar
- Tsp fine sea salt
- Flaked sea salt

You will need 6 x 150ml ramekins (ordinary size in other words). Pour the milk into a small saucepan. Split the vanilla pod lengthways and, using a sharp knife, scrape out the seeds and add to the milk along with the pod. Bring to the boil then remove from the heat and leave to infuse.

To make the caramel, be bold. Place the sugar in a saucepan with 2 tbsp water and the salt. Bring to the boil, stirring now and again until the sugar has dissolved, then simmer for about 10 minutes until it turns a deep toffee-apple gold, stirring as it begins to colour at the edges. Pour this over the bases of the ramekins and leave to harden for about 15 minutes.

Preheat the oven to 150 C. Bring the milk back to the boil. In a separate bowl whisk the eggs and sugar for the custard then stir in the hot milk and pass the mixture through a sieve into a jug. Place the ramekins in a roasting tray and stand this on a baking sheet. Pour the custard evenly on top of the caramel in each ramekin. Put cold water into the roasting tray to come two thirds of the way up the sides of the ramekins. Bake in the oven for 1 - 1 ¼ hours until set. Lift the ramekins from the tray and leave to cool then cover and refrigerate. They will keep well for several days.

To serve, run a knife around the edge of each crème caramel, place a plate on top and turn out on to it. Sprinkle a little flaked sea salt on top of each one to decorate.

UNION JACK MERINGUE
(SERVES 8 - 10)

Food journalists, patriotic souls to the last, quite rightly love to make the most of any special celebratory event - be it Valentine's Day, Easter, the Glorious Twelfth, Halloween etc. The Queen's Jubilee saw the re-emergence of all types of receipts which have dominated her reign. This meringue cake might be viewed as a bit of a Blue Peter type effort but, nonetheless, it's well worth the work given the sighs and murmurs of approval it evokes when brought to the table. As a summer show-stopper, make it when the soft fruits are at their finest. If you have no strawberries to hand, then use raspberries.

- 6 egg whites
- 500g / 1 lb caster sugar
- 400m / 14 fl oz double cream
- ½ tsp vanilla extract
- 500g / 1 lb strawberries
- 500g / 1 lb blueberries

Preheat the oven to 120 C. Select two large baking sheets and cut out two identically sized large rectangles of baking parchment, a bit larger than the flag will be. Mark out the rectangle in pencil on both sheets then outline all the white parts of the Union Jack on one of them - looking at an image of the flag whilst doing so.

In a large, clean bowl beat the egg whites to soft peaks then, still whisking, gradually add half the sugar. Gently fold in the remaining sugar with a large metal spoon. Cut the end of an icing or stiff freezer bag, to make a hole 2 ½ cm/ 1" in diameter or use a plain icing nozzle. Stick the pieces of baking parchment to the sheets with dabs of meringue in each corner. Pipe parallel lines of meringue on to the plain sheet of paper until you have completely filled the area. Then pipe the white cross part of the flag on the other sheet. Bake both in the oven for 1 ½ hours then turn down the oven to its lowest temperature and bake for a further 6 hours or overnight. Leave to cool and harden.

Four hours or less before serving, whip the cream and vanilla extract into floppy peaks. Place the base meringue on a flat platter or cake board and spread most of the cream mix over the base. Gently peel the paper from the meringue cross and place on top of the solid meringue rectangle and cover each baton with the remaining cream. Arrange halved strawberries on the cross shapes and then fill the triangles with the blueberries. Serve with jubilation.

Tips
FROM THE SINK

- The meringue can be made up to 2 weeks in advance and stored in an airtight tin.

Jellies & Ice-Creams

As children, these were the ultimate pudding treats. We dreamt of wibbly-wobbly jellies and iced-frozen delights. Indeed, they also represented the ultimate bribe for 'being good'. And the best place to claim such a reward was the Soda Fountain (now sadly deceased) at Fortnum & Mason. Perched on a high stool at the bar was where I first acquired my penchant for iced-coffee served with a scoop of ice-cream, milk-floats, knickerbocker glories, banana splits and sundaes. Choosing but one was impossible. These childish tastes still prevail so here, for all ages, are some suggestions to keep everyone happy.

RHUBARB AND GINGER JELLIES
(SERVES 6)

This is elegant and easy and can be prepared well in advance. The upside is that there is no need to bother with leaf gelatine as the packet jelly does the work. Ginger, orange and rhubarb are all considered best friends and their flavours marry well here. These look even prettier if made in individual dishes or martini glasses.

- 500g / 1 lb rhubarb stalks, cleaned and chopped into 2" / 5 cm pieces
- Heaped tbsp root ginger, peeled and grated
- 50g / 2 oz caster sugar
- 135g / 5 oz packet orange flavour jelly
- 500ml / 18 fl oz ginger beer (use a good brand not cheapest)
- Mascarpone, to serve
- 3 pieces preserved ginger

Put the rhubarb and sugar in a pan together with the grated ginger and cook gently for approx 12 - 15 minutes until the fruit is soft. It may disintegrate and looked a bit smashed but this doesn't matter.

Whilst that is cooking, break the jelly into squares and put in a jug with 3 tbsp boiling water and leave to dissolve on the side of the Aga (or shove it in microwave). When melted top up with the ginger beer. Next, combine the liquid with the rhubarb and stir together then simply pour into pretty glasses.

Leave to cool then cover and refrigerate to set.

To serve, finely dice the preserved ginger and mix together with the mascarpone and hand round in a bowl.

SLOE GIN JELLIES
(SERVES 12)

Their jewel-like colour makes these a dazzling dessert and a fitting one also for the Christmas table.

- 8 - 9 gelatine leaves
- 500ml / 18 fl oz sloe gin
- 500ml / 18 fl oz cranberry juice
- Juice of a lemon

To make the jellies, soak the gelatine leaves in a basin of cold water for 10 minutes. Meanwhile, mix the sloe gin, cranberry and lemon juices in a large jug and ladle a cupful of this liquid into a small pan and heat gently. When the gelatine leaves are soft, squeeze all the water from them and stir them into the warm liquid. Once the leaves have completely dissolved, return this liquid to the rest of the sloe gin mixture and pour into individual glasses or pretty small china tea cups (these need not match) and leave to cool, then cover and refrigerate until set.

PIMM'S JELLIES

A light and sophisticated way of enjoying Pimm's in a glass.

- 5 gelatine leaves
- 110g / 4 oz caster sugar
- 100ml / 3 ½ fl oz water
- 100ml / 3 ½ fl oz lemonade or ginger ale or half of each
- 175ml / 6 fl oz Pimm's
- 250g / 8 oz strawberries, hulled and thinly sliced
- ¼ cucumber, peeled, seeded and finely diced
- Handful of mint leaves, finely chopped, plus sprigs to serve

Put the gelatine leaves into a basin of cold water and soak for 10 minutes to soften.

Place the sugar and water into a saucepan over a medium-low heat, stirring constantly until the sugar has dissolved. Remove from the heat and stir in the softened gelatine leaves from which you have squeezed all the water.

Transfer the mixture to a bowl and add the Pimm's and lemonade/ginger ale.

Arrange some of the strawberries and cucumber in the base of four small glasses and pour over some of the liquid to cover. Allow to set in the fridge for 15 minutes then add the next layer and once more, leave to set. Repeat the process until all the ingredients have been used up. Decorate with sprigs of mint and serve with macaroons, now available in all good supermarkets.

SUE'S COFFEE ICE CREAM

Sue Clark produced this at the end of dinner after an epic day's hunting with the Wynnstay. So exhausted were we all that everyone protested they couldn't eat another mouthful. Needless to say, we licked the platter clean. No discredit to Sue but it is a doddle to make.

- 450ml / ¾ pint double cream
- 225g / 7 fl oz condensed milk
- 4 tbsp Camp coffee
- Kahlúa coffee liqueur to taste (optional)

Whip the cream to soft peaks. Whisk in all the other ingredients and freeze.

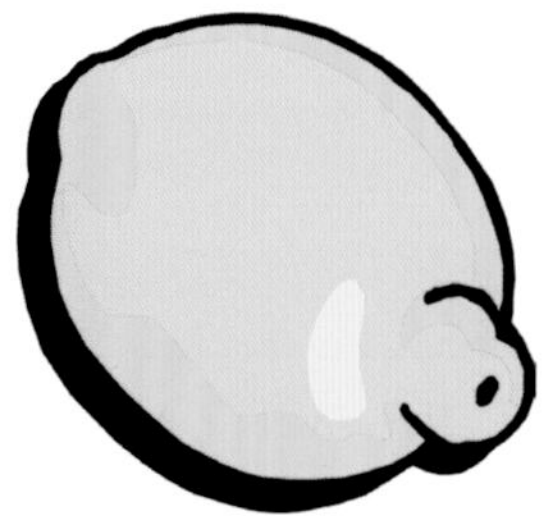

LEMON CURD ICE CREAM

- 300 ml / ½ pint whipping cream
- 225g / 7 fl oz Greek yoghurt
- Jar lemon curd
- Zest and juice of a lemon
- 4 meringues (shop bought are fine) lightly crushed

Whip the cream until it forms soft peaks. Add the yoghurt and meringues then stir in the curd, zest and juice. Freeze for an hour then remove mixture and beat well before returning to the deep freeze. Take out to soften before serving.

AFFOGATO

This is something I order in restaurants when I am trying to pretend to myself that I don't want a pudding but the reality is that I do. I really do! It is like a simple ice cream sundae for grown- ups and relies on the strength of the coffee used, ideally espresso. Put a scoop of best quality vanilla ice-cream (it must be very hard) into a coffee cup or small bowl and pour a small amount of very strong, i.e. double espresso - hot coffee over the top and serve immediately.

CRUNCHIE ICE CREAM

(SERVES 8)

- 5 Crunchie bars
- 400g / 14 fl oz condensed milk
- 300 ml / ½ pint double cream, whipped to soft folds

Lightly oil a loaf tin or a bowl then line with clingfilm. Put the Crunchie bars into a polythene bag and secure the top then bash with a rolling pin so that you end up with small pieces and shards. In a large bowl, whip the double cream, then pour in the condensed milk and finally mix in the crunchie bits. Transfer to the loaf tin or bowl and place in the deep freeze for several hours until frozen.

VELVET CHOCOLATE TORTE
(SERVES 8)

This takes 10 minutes to make and is great to have in the freezer – it goes brilliantly with poached fruit and seasonal berries.

- 200g / 7 oz good quality dark chocolate
- 100g / 4 oz caster sugar
- 125 ml / 4 fl oz water
- 4 egg yolks
- 2 tbsp brandy
- 586ml / 1 pint double cream

Line a loose-bottomed or spring-form tin (approx 20cm / 8" diameter) with cling film. Break the chocolate into squares and drop in the bowl of the food processor. Blitz for a minute or two until just a few small pieces remain and the rest is like a powdery chocolate. Measure the sugar and water into a saucepan and heat gently until the sugar has dissolved then raise the heat and boil briskly for approx 4 minutes to obtain a thin syrup. Set the processor running and pour this liquid through the funnel onto the chocolate so that it melts. Add just a tad more boiling water if some of the chocolate hasn't melted. Next, add the egg yolks and process for a few seconds then tip in the brandy.

In a separate bowl, beat the cream to form soft, floppy folds – not butter (!) then fold in the chocolate and transfer to the tin. Cover with cling and freeze for at least 4 hours.

To serve, remove from the freezer at least 20 - 25 minutes before serving and turn out onto a plate. Sift a little icing sugar over the surface and hand round with Raspberry Sauce (page 225).

SEVILLE ORANGE ICED CREAM WITH DARK CHOCOLATE SAUCE

(SERVES 8 - 10)

- 3 Seville oranges, well scrubbed under cold water, then dried
- 300ml / ½ pint double cream
- 100g / 4 oz icing sugar, sifted
- 4 eggs, separated

Sauce:

- 150g / 6 oz granulated sugar
- 150ml / ¼ pint boiling water
- Tsp vanilla essence
- 3 tbsp cocoa, sieved
- 3 tbsp golden syrup
- 25g / 1 oz butter

To make the iced cream, zest and juice the oranges and set both aside. Whip the cream in a large bowl until it forms soft peaks, at which stage gradually pour in the Seville juice. In a separate bowl, whip the egg whites until stiff and then, continuing to whisk, add half the sieved icing sugar. Next, whisk the egg yolks with the remaining icing sugar and the orange zest until the mixture is creamy and thick. Using a metal spoon, fold into the whipped cream and gently ensure it is evenly mixed. Turn into a large container and freeze.

For the chocolate sauce, place all the ingredients into a saucepan and heat until the sugar has completely dissolved, stirring constantly then bring to the boil for 4 - 5 minutes - the longer it boils, the more fudge-like its consistency. Cover and store in the fridge then reheat to serve with the iced cream which has been thawed in the fridge for at least 30 minutes before dishing up.

THE BRIG'S LEMON SORREL SORBET

If I were Peter Rabbit, I would definitely make a beeline for Andrew Parker Bowles's vegetable garden. Discreetly tucked away behind a post and rails fence which, throughout the summer, is smothered in heavenly scented and blousy sweet-peas (from specialist producer Roger Parsons), the rows of produce are organised and grown with military precision. Hardly surprising when you consider Andrew's own army background and his inherited gardening skills. His great uncle was the highly revered and still celebrated E.A. Bowles, - horticulturist, plantsman and garden writer whose name has been preserved in many types of plants. The Brig's own name may not (yet!) be formally recognised with anything from his potager although his French lemon sorrel which originated from Sue Dickinson, head gardener at Waddesden Manor, could put him in the winner's enclosure. This receipt is adapted from the version served at The Woodspeen Restaurant which has undoubtedly raised the cooking stakes in West Berkshire. Any variety of sorrel will work successfully here.

Syrup:

- 300ml / ½ pint water
- 150g / 6 oz caster sugar
- 40ml / 1 ½ fl oz glucose

Sorbet:

- 300g / 10 oz sorrel leaves, picked over, de-veined and finely chopped
- 600ml / 1 pint sorbet syrup
- 500g / just under 1 pint natural yoghurt

For the syrup, put all the ingredients in a saucepan and bring to a simmer for 2 minutes. Do not boil. Chill before using.

To make the sorbet, blend the syrup with the sorrel until smooth, then pass through a sieve. Whisk in the yoghurt and blend thoroughly to emulsify. Churn in an ice cream machine and freeze until required.

Baking

It's official. Baking is 'on trend' so go dust down the muffin tins and find, or perhaps invent, your inner-self by whipping up sponges and the like. The Great British Bake Off has sparked a national renaissance in terms of 'there will be cake for tea' and continues to create a whole new panoply of glorious treats. And the contestants don't stop dreaming up new ways involving eggs, sugar and flour as the standard rises and rises with yet more unusual ingredients going into their mixing bowls to produce exotic and previously unheard of combinations. They've got the rest of us drooling and so, on that note, 'on your marks, get set, bake'!

ROSEMARY'S FRUITCAKE

Rosemary is a great friend of my mother's and I have often thought that between them they could give some of the participants in the Great British Bake Off a run for their money. They come from an era when there was unfailingly cake for tea and perhaps not just one but several different varieties.

- 250g / 8 oz mixed fruit
- 100g / 4 oz cherries, halved
- 100g / 4 oz dried apricots, chopped
- 100ml / 2 ½ fl oz sherry
- 100g / 4 oz butter, softened or margarine
- 100g / 4 oz dark brown sugar
- 25g / 1 oz chopped almonds
- 50g / 2 oz each self-raising flour and plain flour, mixed together
- 2 eggs
- ½ tsp mixed spice
- Tsp salt
- Tbsp black treacle

Preheat the oven to 150 C and prepare a 6" square tin or 7" round tin, by buttering and lining it with baking paper.

Soak the mixed fruits, cherries and apricots with the sherry overnight - either in the airing cupboard, on top of the boiler or by the Aga!

Cream the butter or margarine and sugar together. Add eggs and gradually stir in all dry ingredients plus treacle. Finally add fruit and chopped almonds and mix well. Bake for 1 ½ hours and then reduce the heat to 140 C and cook for a further 45 minutes. If the top becomes too brown, cover with baking paper.

SPICED TOFFEE APPLE CAKE

A Bonfire Night inspired cake with its own twist on traditional toffee apples.

- 200g / 7 oz pitted dates, roughly chopped
- 200ml / 7 fl oz milk, plus a splash
- 250g / 8 oz butter, softened, plus extra for greasing
- 275g / 9 oz self-raising flour
- 200g / 7 oz light soft brown sugar
- ½ tsp baking powder
- 4 eggs
- Tsp ground cinnamon
- Tbsp ground mixed spice
- 2 tsp vanilla extract
- 4 small red apples
- Squeeze lemon juice
- Icing sugar

Sauce:

- 300ml/ ½ pint double cream
- 2 tbsp golden syrup
- 100g / 4 oz soft brown sugar

Preheat the oven to 180 C. Grease and line a 20 x 30 cm baking tray with baking parchment. Put the dates and milk in a small pan and bring to a simmer then remove from the heat and leave to stand until cool. Whizz the date mixture to a smooth purée in a food processor then transfer into a large mixing bowl. Tip in the butter, flour, brown sugar, baking powder, eggs, cinnamon, mixed spice and vanilla and set aside. To prepare the apples, peel, quarter and core then slice quite thinly, tossing in a little lemon juice as you go. Quickly beat the cake ingredients together with an electric whisk until smooth then scrape into the baking tray. Arrange the apple slices, overlapping in rows, on top of the mixture and bake for 45 - 50 minutes until a skewer comes out clean. Cool in the tray.

For the fudge sauce, heat the three ingredients in a pan and stir until entirely smooth.

To serve, dust the cake with icing sugar, then drizzle the sauce all over then slice.

MARY BALL'S WASHINGTON GINGERBREAD

Years ago, when milkmen did their daily rounds in their then familiar electric floats, and the bottles our daily pint came in were all made of glass, a wonderful book called 'The Dairy Book of Family Cookery' also arrived on the doorstep one day. It was at this time my initial interest in cooking had been ignited so I was hungry for ideas and receipts that were do-able for a hesitant learner. This was one of the first cakes I ever baked and, as its name suggests, it is an old American one attributed to the mother of the famous President of the USA. I can still remember now being very chuffed with the results. No food writer can better giving a cook confidence.

- 100g / 4 oz butter, softened
- 100g / 4 oz soft brown sugar
- Tsp cream of tartar
- 150g / 6 oz sultanas
- 150ml / 5 fl oz milk, warmed
- 3 tbsp sherry
- 2 tbsp ground ginger
- Grated zest of an orange
- Tsp bicarbonate of soda, dissolved in 2 tbsp warm water
- 2 tsp ground cinnamon
- 3 tsp freshly grated nutmeg
- 5 cubes preserved ginger, diced
- 225g / 8 oz golden syrup
- 100g / 4 oz treacle
- 3 eggs

Preheat the oven to 160 C. Grease two square 18cm / 7" baking tins and line with greased greaseproof or non-stick silicone paper. In a bowl cream the butter and sugar together until light and fluffy. Sift the flour with the cream of tartar into a separate bowl and add the sultanas. In a third bowl combine the milk, sherry, spices, ginger, golden syrup, treacle and eggs. Fold the flour mixture alternatively with the milk and spice mixture into the creamed butter and sugar. Beat all well until thoroughly combined. Finally beat in the orange zest and dissolved bicarbonate of soda.

Pour the mixture into the prepare tins and bake in the oven for 30 minutes then reduce the temperature to 150 C and cook for a further 30 - 40 minutes. Leave to cool in the tins then turn out on to a wire rack.

THE QUEEN MOTHER'S FAVOURITE CAKE

I found this hand-written receipt lurking within a book I picked up in a junk shop, headed thus. The piece of paper is signed 'Good Luck - from Nancy'. So Nancy, to you I must say 'Thank You'. Some of the ingredients are measured in a cup. As long as you use the same cup for everything, it works out perfectly. Just don't vary the size!

- Cup boiling water
- Cup pitted dates, chopped
- Tsp bicarbonate of soda
- Cup of caster sugar
- Egg, beaten
- ½ cup chopped walnuts
- ½ cup (approx 65g/ 2 1/2 oz) butter
- Tsp vanilla essence
- Tsp baking powder
- ½ tsp salt

Topping:

- 5 tbsp brown sugar
- 2 tbsp butter, softened
- 2 tbsp cream

Preheat the oven to 175 - 180 C and grease a 9" x 12" tin. Put the dates into a large bowl and pour over the boiling water. Add the bicarbonate of soda and leave this to stand whilst you mix the next set of ingredients below then add these to the dates and combine. Bake for 35-40 minutes.

Mix the topping ingredients together in a saucepan and boil for 3 minutes. When you have removed the cake from the oven allow to cool and then spread with this icing. Chopped toasted nuts may also be added if wished.

BARM BRACK TEA LOAF

Another of my first baking efforts. In other words, idiot proof!

- 450ml / ¾ pint cold tea
- 175g / 7 oz soft brown sugar
- 350g / 12 oz mixed dried fruit
- 300g / 10 oz self-raising flour
- Egg, beaten

Put the tea, sugar and dried fruit in a bowl, cover and leave overnight to soak.

Preheat the oven to 180 C and grease a 2lb loaf tin. Mix the soaked fruit etc with the flour. Add the beaten egg and mix until smooth. Bake for approximately 1 ¾ hours and when cool turn out onto a wire rack. Serve sliced with butter and, if wished, jam.

BLACKBERRY AND BROWN SUGAR LOAF

A good tea time loaf and ideal, also, for picnics. If you are making this out of the blackberry (bramble) picking season, use blueberries instead.

- 175g / 6 oz unsalted butter
- 175g / 6 oz light brown sugar
- 2 eggs, well beaten
- 2 heaped tbsp sour cream
- Tbsp grated lemon zest
- Pinch of ground cinnamon
- 250g / 8 oz plain flour, sifted
- Tsp baking powder
- 200g / 7 oz blackberries
- Icing sugar, for dusting

Preheat the oven to 180 C. Beat the butter and sugar until light and fluffy. Add one tablespoon of the flour and the eggs gradually, beating until creamy. Turn down the speed of the mixer and add the sour cream, lemon zest, cinnamon and flour. Beat until the mixture just comes together. Sift the baking powder over the top, sprinkle on the blackberries and gently fold into the mixture, breaking them up as little as possible. Spoon the batter into a buttered loaf tin(standard size 23 x 13 cm / 9" x 5"), smooth the top and bake until a skewer inserted comes out clean - test after around 25 minutes. Leave to cool and then turn out onto a wire rack. Dust with icing sugar before serving.

EASTER CHOCOLATE BROWNIES

My mother, a dedicated baker, religiously bakes me a simnel cake every Easter but I have never dared ask for her receipt for fear that she might then tell me to make my own. Only very honoured friends are ever offered a slice. These swirled chocolate brownies, paired with a caramel cheesecake, are easy to make. Finished off with Cadbury's Mini Eggs, they look suitably festive.

- 150g / 6 oz butter plus extra for greasing
- 150g / 6 oz dark chocolate, roughly chopped
- 50g / 2 oz dark muscovado sugar
- ½ tsp vanilla extract
- Tsp cornflour
- 4 eggs
- 200g / 7 oz cream cheese
- 200g / 7 oz light muscovado sugar
- 75g / 3 oz plain flour
- Bag Cadbury's Mini Eggs

Preheat the oven to 180 C. Grease and line a 20cm / 9" square tin with baking parchment. Place the butter and chocolate in a heatproof bowl and set over a pan of gently simmering water, stirring occasionally, until melted. Alternatively, stand the bowl on the Aga.

For the cheesecake mixture, beat together the dark muscovado sugar, vanilla extract, cornflour and 1 egg. Gently stir in the cream cheese until combined and set aside.

Beat the remaining 3 eggs in a bowl. Stir in the chocolate mixture with the light muscovado sugar and the flour. Spoon half of this into the tin, then drop in small spoonfuls of the cheesecake mixture. Cover with the remaining chocolate mixture and, using a skewer or fork, lightly ripple the top. Bake in the oven for 20 minutes, then remove and scatter over the Mini Eggs and return to the heat for a further 15 minutes or so until cooked. Leave to cool in the tin before cutting into squares.

HAZELNUT SHORTBREAD

- 100g / 4 oz unsalted butter
- 100g / 4 oz icing sugar, sifted
- 2 egg yolks
- 50g / 2 oz whole hazelnuts, dry roasted and ground up in processor
- 350g / 12 oz plain flour, sifted

Pre-heat the oven to 180 C. Cream together the butter and icing sugar then add the egg yolks and mix well. Stir in the flour and bring together to form a ball of dough. Wrap in cling film or greaseproof paper and leave to rest in the fridge for an hour or so.

Roll out on a floured surface to a thickness of 3 - 4mm and, using a cutter, stamp into rounds. Place these on a baking sheet bake the biscuits in the oven for approximately 10 - 12 minutes or until a golden brown.

Tips FROM THE SINK

- Use these during the strawberry season to make a pudding. Add the fruit - sliced - to whipped cream and sandwich between two biscuits. Sieve over a little icing sugar and decorate the top of each one with a half strawberry.

Baking

PENNY'S CHOCOLATE BISCUITS

Penny Lindsay-Fynn lives in County Meath and I am a regular visitor to their lovely house Carrollstown which I look upon as my Irish home! It is always filled with friends, family and fun. Penny serves these biscuits alongside puddings such as fruit salads, mousses and jellies as well as together with ice-cream and sorbets.

- 250g / 8 oz unsalted butter, softened
- 200g / 6 oz caster sugar
- 300g / 10 oz self-raising flour
- 25g / 1 oz cocoa
- Tbsp drinking chocolate
- Water to mix

Preheat the oven to 180 C. Sieve the flour, cocoa and drinking chocolate together into bowl. Cream the butter and sugar then add the flour, cocoa and drinking chocolate and mix until it forms a coarse mixture. Add a teaspoon of water or more as necessary. Pat into small balls and press down onto a baking sheet with a fork. Bake for 8 - 10 minutes, watching carefully. Leave to cool and harden on the baking tray before storing in a tin until required. Sprinkle with icing sugar to serve.

Tips FROM THE SINK

- This is quite a large quantity of mixture so either halve it or freeze the rest to cook another time.
- A couple of lumps of sugar placed inside a tin help to keep the biscuits dry and crisp.

CHOCOLATE FRIDGE CAKE

The ultimate and totally irresistible sweet-treat indulgence. As a child I made a simpler version of this which went into the tuckbox for the dreaded return to school. This is more sophisticated and every Christmas I make copious numbers of these as part of my **Dishes With Dashers** *foods I offer for sale and also as presents.*

- 250g / 8 oz best quality dark chocolate (70% + cocoa solids)
- 100g / 4 oz butter
- Tbsp golden or maple syrup
- 100g / 4 oz Rich Tea, Digestive or plain Hobnob biscuits
- 75g / 3 oz amaretti biscuits
- 100g / 4 oz whole almonds, lightly toasted and roughly chopped
- 50g / 2 oz pistachio nuts, shelled
- 50g / 2 oz marshmallows, chopped
- 3 pieces preserved ginger, neatly diced
- Assorted chocolate bars - KitKat, Crunchie, Snickers, Crunchie, Mars - chopped
- 3 tbsp kirsch
- 3 tbsp morello cherries, drained

Wet the inside of an ordinary-sized loaf tin (mine takes just under one litre / 2 pints water when filled) and line with cling film. Melt the chocolate, butter and syrup together either in a heatproof bowl set over a pan of barely simmering water or put the ingredients in a bowl and stand on the Aga. Stir to ensure it is completely smooth. Break the biscuits and amaretti into smallish pieces then add to the chocolate mixture along with everything else and combine then transfer to the loaf tin. Press down well and bring the cling film over the top to cover. Place in the fridge for a few hours. When you are ready to eat this, turn it out onto a flat plate or board and slice.

CHENDA'S FLORENTINES

To many of you Richenda, who originally quipped the phrase 'Tips from the Sink' when acting during our cookery demos as my helper (though she preferred to call herself the scullery maid Ruby), needs no introduction. She produced these divine florentines one day telling me that the original receipt came from Mrs Simms, the fat, old cook at Bowood. Well, we would all be that shape if we ate these continuously. They make a brilliant present if you can bear to part with any.

- 85g / 3½ oz butter
- 100g / 4 oz caster sugar
- 100g / 4 oz chopped nuts - walnuts, almonds and/or hazelnuts
- 2 tbsp sultanas, chopped
- Tbsp glacé cherries, chopped
- 2 tbsp mixed peel, chopped
- Tbsp double cream

Coating:

- 150g / 6 oz dark chocolate
- 25g / 1 oz butter

Preheat the oven to 180 C. Melt the butter and sugar in a saucepan and bring to the boil for about one minute. Stir in the remaining ingredients and put teaspoons of the mixture on a non-stick baking tray. Remember they will spread out during cooking so don't overcrowd. Cook for 10 minutes, pushing up using a palette knife once or twice during the process.

When golden, remove from the heat and leave to cool a little before carefully transferring them to a wire rack. Continue cooking the rest of the batch until the mixture is all used. Meanwhile, for the coating, melt the chocolate and butter together and keep warmed until required. Once the florentines are cold and set, paint the backs with the chocolate. Store carefully between sheets of greaseproof paper and keep in an airtight container in the fridge until required.

CHEESE SCONES

My sister Jane was sent to London to do a cookery course in Wimbledon with Elizabeth Russell. I always felt I was the loser having been made to do a thoroughly cheerless secretarial course. Even then, high speeds at the typewriter and in Pitman's shorthand seemed a dull way of spending the days when, instead, one could have been in the kitchen honing baking skills. These scones go especially well with soups.

- 250g / 8 oz self-raising flour
- 3 level tsp baking powder
- Pinch paprika
- Pinch salt
- 50g / 2 oz margarine or butter
- 100g / 4 oz strong cheese - i.e. Cheddar, Gruyère or Comté, grated
- 150ml / ¼ pint milk, plus a little extra for glazing

Preheat the oven to 200 C. Sieve the flour, baking powder, paprika and salt into a bowl. Rub in the fat until the mixture resembles fine breadcrumbs then add the cheese. Pour in the milk and mix with a fork. Knead the dough lightly until it is smooth and, using a cutter, shape into rounds. Brush the tops with milk and bake for 10 - 12 minutes until pale golden in colour and hollow when tapped. Stand on a wire tray and leave to cool.

Canapés

As a rule of thumb, I always rather dread having to make canapés. All that fiddle and faff which reached its zenith when miniaturisation of fish 'n' chips, beef Wellingtons, hamburgers, eggs Benedict etc became rampant! If the truth be told, I'm full of admiration for caterers, and indeed friends, who can produce tray upon tray of tempting treats – elegant morsels rather like edible art on a plate. My own party food, made as it is, minus an army of sous-chefs and helpers, veers towards simpler morsels. One of my best secret weapons which I rely upon hugely are a good stash of those croustade cases you can buy in supermarkets. The trick though is to put them out onto a baking sheet and place in a hot oven for a few minutes then leave them to cool as this will crisp them up and stop them going soggy once filled. Also best to leave them until just before serving until you fill them. Try them with Potted Shrimps (page 39).

TOASTED ROSEMARY & SEA SALT NUTS

These are wickedly good and great to have as a standby - I try and keep a read-made stash in a jar.

- 350g / 12 oz mixed nuts, unsalted
- 2 tbsp rosemary leaves, roughly chopped
- Scant tsp cayenne pepper
- 2 tsp dark brown sugar
- 2 tsp Maldon sea salt
- Tbsp butter, melted

Heat a large non-stick frying pan until hot then tip in the nuts and toast until just golden brown giving the pan the odd shake to move them around. Watch them carefully as they can catch and burn very quickly. In a large bowl combine the rosemary, cayenne, sugar, salt and melted butter then add the nuts to coat them. Best served warm but still very good when cold.

PARMESAN CRISPS

I love these delicate lacy biscuits because they look so much cleverer than they actually are. I also offer them with soups or as a garnish to a starter-style salad.

- Large chunk of finest Parmesan, finely grated

Press the finely grated cheese into small balls. Place two or three in a hot, dry, non-stick frying pan and, using the blade of a knife, gently press out and flatten to a medium-sized disc. Leave on the heat until they are crisp then transfer to kitchen towel and continue cooking the rest.

FOUR BY FOUR CHEESE HEARTS

Handy to have stored in a tin and also a good accompaniment to soups. Alternatively, heat through and serve as a savoury.

- 100g / 4 oz plain flour
- 100g / 4 oz cold butter, diced into cubes
- 50g / 2 oz Parmesan, finely grated
- 50g / 2 oz mature Cheddar, grated
- Generous pinch cayenne pepper
- Tsp mustard powder
- Egg, beaten

Preheat the oven to 180 C. Whizz the flour and butter together in a food processor to resemble fine breadcrumbs then blitz in the two cheeses, cayenne pepper and mustard powder until the mixture comes together to form a ball. Remove from the bowl, wrap in cling film and refrigerate for at least 30 minutes. (This can also be frozen). Roll out the dough onto a floured surface to a thickness of at least ½ cm but not too thin. Using a cutter, stamp out into chosen shape - i.e. hearts, discs etc and put on a non-stick baking tray, reasonably spaced apart. Brush each one with the egg and cook for approx 12 minutes until golden brown.

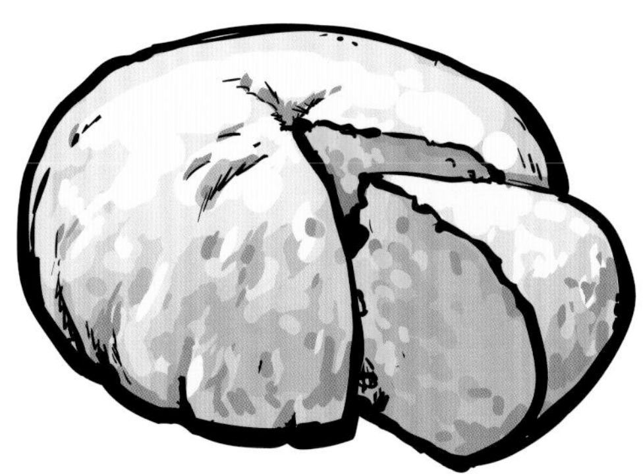

ROASTED ASPARAGUS WRAPPED IN PARMA HAM

- 24 asparagus spears, trimmed
- 12 slices Parma ham
- Olive oil
- Balsamic vinegar
- Seasoning

Preheat the oven to 190 C. Lay the ham slices, one at a time, on a board or flat surface and cut each one in half lengthways. Roll each spear neatly in a piece of ham and place on an oiled parchment paper or a Bake-O-Glide liner. Season with salt and freshly ground white pepper. Shake over the olive oil and a few shakes of balsamic vinegar and roast in the oven for 10 minutes or so until the ham is crispy and the asparagus has softened to the touch.

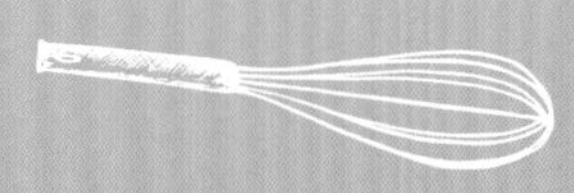

Tips FROM THE SINK

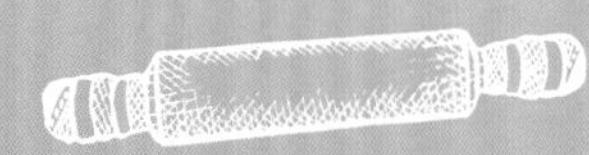

- Also an excellent starter. Place a few of these wands on individual plates on top of assorted, lightly dressed salad leaves and add a few shavings of Parmesan to each one.

FRIED FINGERS WITH MOZZARELLA AND PROSCIUTTO

Fried sandwiches are quick and easy and make a delicious hot bite to have with a cocktail or to hand round before lunch.

- 200ml / 7 fl oz milk
- 6 slices decent white bread, crusts removed
- Ball of mozzarella, drained and cut into thin slices
- Seasoning
- 3 - 4 slices prosciutto
- 2 - 3 tbsp olive oil

Pour the milk into a bowl and dip the bread in briefly so it is damp but not soggy. Place slices of the mozzarella on a slice of bread and season with black pepper then lay over a slice of prosciutto, tearing it to fit. Place another piece of milk bread on top to form a sandwich and press together.

Heat enough olive oil to coat the base of a heavy non-stick frying pan and when the oil is hot, fry the sandwiches for a minute or so until golden. You may need to reduce the heat a little to prevent them from burning, then flip over and cook the other side - about another minute or two. Transfer to kitchen paper to absorb any excess oil and place on a board and cut into wide fingers. Serve immediately.

CHERRY'S PRAWN BITES

I am passionate about these. With their kick of chilli they can assert themselves through a babble-filled room and will hot-up the party nicely. So-called because Cherry Jones asked me, when attending a ***Dishes With Dashers*** *cooking demo, to include a new canapé. This is what I came up with.*

- 250g / 8 oz cooked shelled prawns, drained and patted dry on kitchen paper
- Small red chilli, seeded and finely chopped
- Handful coriander leaves, chopped
- Grated zest of lemon or lime
- Stalk lemongrass, outer layer removed and remainder finely chopped
- 2 garlic cloves, crushed
- Heaped tbsp plain flour
- Groundnut or sunflower oil

To serve:

- Sweet chilli jam/dipping sauce or homemade Mayonnaise (page 216)

Simply put all the ingredients, bar the oil, into a food processor and pulse until well mixed but still with a bit of texture. You don't want a total wet mush! Press into bite-size patties, put onto a plate and chill in the fridge for approx 30 minutes. Heat the oil in a large non-stick frying pan and when hot, sauté the 'cakes' on one side until nicely browned (approx a minute) and then flip over and cook on the other side. Remove and blot on kitchen paper and serve with sweet chilli jam/dipping sauce (available from all supermarkets).

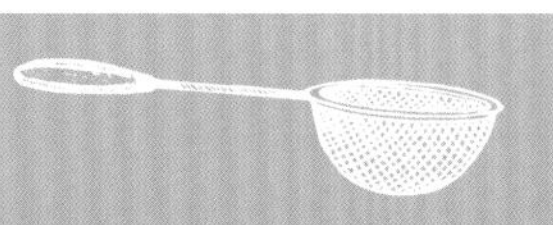

Tips FROM THE SINK

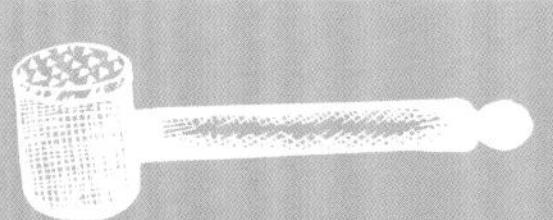

- Try replacing the prawns with some fresh crab meat, both white and brown. These also make excellent full-size fish cakes to serve as a main course for 4 people.

COD'S ROE DIP

A far cry from the tubs of 'Disneyland Pink' found on supermarket shelves which bear no resemblance in either appearance or flavour to the properly made version here.

- 250g / 8 oz smoked cod's roe
- 200ml / ⅓ pint groundnut oil
- 50ml / 3 fl oz olive oil
- Juice of a lemon
- Cayenne pepper
- Twist or three black pepper

Skin the cod's roe and whizz in a food processor then trickle in the oils and lemon juice. Add seasoning followed by 2 – 3 tbsp cold water to make it creamy and blitz once more. Taste to check it has enough lemon then transfer to a bowl and serve with breadsticks, oven-baked slices of baguette or on toasted sourdough. Finish off with a sprinkling of cayenne pepper.

MALT LOAF SMOKED SALMON

Smoked salmon on brown, soda, rye and pumpernickel breads are commonplace. Try piling it on top of malted loaf or my Barm Brack Tea Loaf (page 162) lavishly spread with cream or ricotta cheese. Finish off with a squeeze of lemon juice, plenty of black pepper and a scattering of cress.

FIONA BROWNE'S PRAWN 'N' CHEESE TOASTS

Fiona Browne runs a fantastically successful clothes business 'Browne and Daughters' which typifies style and elegance. She echoes these traits when it comes to hosting excellent parties. Together with her husband, their Christmas Eve Drinks Party is a seamless flow of deliciousness canapés being offered round. I seem to recall doing justice to an ungainly number of these - but these were definitely the 'dish of the day' - well, evening.

- 100g / 4 oz shelled cooked prawns, roughly chopped
- 4 tbsp mayonnaise - I use Hellmann's
- 100g / 4 oz Parmesan, finely grated
- Seasoning
- Worcester sauce, to taste
- 4 slices brown bread, toasted on one side, cut into bite-size pieces

Heat the grill to maximum heat. In a bowl, mix the first five ingredients together well. Place the bread on a baking tray, toasted side downwards, and divide the mixture amongst the pieces. Place the tray under the grill and cook until golden brown and bubbling. Transfer to a large serving platter and hand round immediately.

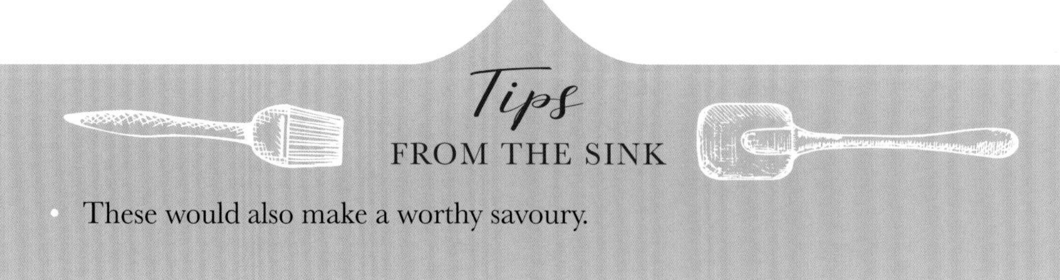

Tips
FROM THE SINK

- These would also make a worthy savoury.

GOUJONS OF PHEASANT

Chicken nuggets eat your heart out! This answers that perennial cry of 'what shall we do with all the pheasant' and makes either an excellent canapé or first course.

- 3 - 4 large clean (i.e. devoid of shot) pheasant breasts, skinned
- White breadcrumbs - approx 5 large slices bread, crusts removed
- 2 - 3 eggs, beaten and seasoned
- Olive oil and butter for sautéeing
- Seasoning

Using a sharp knife, cut the meat into strips and dunk these in a dish containing the eggs to which seasoning has also been added. Toss around until well coated then transfer to the dish containing the breadcrumbs. Heat the olive oil and butter in a large frying pan and when hot, fry off the goujons until nicely browned all over then blot on kitchen paper.

To serve, place the goujons on a bed of lightly dressed rocket leaves and hand round with the beetroot pesto or alternatively Cumberland / Aioli sauce (pages 206 and 215 respectively).

Beetroot Pesto:

- 250g / 8 oz packet vacuum sealed cooked beetroot
- 50g / 2 oz pine nuts, lightly toasted
- 3 - 4 tbsp olive oil
- 50g / 2 oz Parmesan, finely grated
- Seasoning

Roughly chop the beetroot by hand then put in a food processor and blitz to chop further but don't turn into a total purée. Add the nuts and pulse, then pour in a steady stream of olive oil through the funnel. Next, briefly blend in the cheese, check seasoning and if necessary, add more oil to achieve desired consistency.

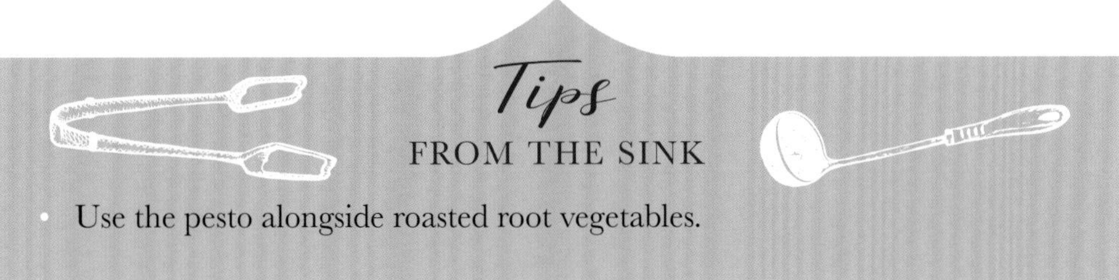

- Use the pesto alongside roasted root vegetables.

The Cocktail Bar

Cocktails have made a spirited comeback in recent times. Once perceived as fashionable drinks, their popularity then dipped but nowadays the heady glamour they represent is right back in vogue as bartenders have resurrected and reformulated some of the blasts from the past, revelling once more in the art of mixology.

Whether shaken or stirred, muddled or served 'straight up', what every cocktail should exude, in essence, is style and finesse. Indeed, what epitomises an elegant lifestyle more than sipping a lovingly created cocktail. There is no finer 'pick-me-up', aperitif, pre-prandial or 'morning after' cure. So, let's toast their success, drown out any sorrows and be prepared to weave around like snipe.

FRENCH 75

For me, the best thing about the Game Fair is not the dizzying array of shops including the Millionaire's Row packed, end to end, cheek by jowl with exotic gun makers, nor the endless demonstrations one can watch. No, it is the highly coveted invitation to The Field magazine's 'French 75' Cocktail Party. First, there is the annual intrigue as to what vivid coloured trousers Editor Jonathan Young will be wearing to dazzle his guests with (I know of no other man whose wardrobe could rival his for its psychedelic hues- such exoticism) and then there are his attempts - usually very successful - to inebriate and intoxicate his guests. French 75's were a favoured stiffener of the Royal Flying Corps. Their kick was likened to shellfire from the French 75mm Howitzer. Trust me, these really do give you wings.

For individual serving:

- Gin, to taste
- Tsp superfine sugar
- Tsp lemon juice
- Glass of Champagne

Shake well with cracked ice in a chilled cocktail shaker, then strain into a tall glass half-full of cracked ice then top off with more Champagne.

DIRTY KITTY

Kitty Fisher's restaurant, found in the heart of London's historic Mayfair, in Shepherd Market, is named after the 18th Century courtesan. Kitty Fisher doesn't muck around - she serves proper drinks.

- Gin
- Sloe gin
- Elderflower
- Lemon Juice
- Prosecco

I will leave the exact quantities to the individual - my only advice is 'go easy on the lemon juice' and serve in tall glasses.

RHUBARB PROSECCO

Prosecco has rocketed in popularity and much of what is produced is now very well made. For my money, it is in a different league to cheap tasting cava and Crémant de Crémant. Serve well chilled and pour into glasses then add a slick of rhubarb juice (leftover from baking this fruit - see page 139) or, if you have none to hand, use sloe gin or vodka - just enough to turn it to a pale pink colour. Excellent as a pre-prandial cocktail.

LEMON VODKA

This is best kept in the fridge or deep freeze.

- 6 lemons
- Lime
- 250g / ½ lb golden granulated sugar
- 250g / ½ lb golden caster sugar
- 1.5 litres / 2½ - 2¾ pints vodka - use a decent brand

Grate the zest of the lemons and lime. Slice 4 of the lemons and lime and put with the sugars in a pan. Add around a quarter of the vodka and dissolve the sugars over a gentle heat. Do not boil. When the sugars have dissolved, add the rest of the lemons (also sliced) and the remaining vodka. Leave to cool, cover and stand in the larder for 4 days pushing the fruit down at regular intervals with a wooden spoon. Strain and bottle.

LUIGI'S VODKA FIZZES

The world-famous Cresta Run in St Moritz is not for the faint-hearted. This is their speciality, originally finessed by a keen tasting committee supervised by popular member, Fernando Rueda and made accordingly, by Luigi, who runs the bar in the Club House of the St Moritz Tobogganing Club. Riding that 'Run' is thirsty work, to mention nothing of the partying which follows. Cresta contestants remain fit by dancing the nights away at Dracs Club.

- 4 - 5 ice cubes
- Tbsp lemon juice
- ½ tbsp liquid glucose sugar
- 2 tbsp vodka

Shake the ingredients together vigorously for at least 50 seconds - the importance of this being to attract everyone's attention!

CRESTA BULLSHOT

The perfect cold weather drink. The Cresta version of this is always served in the changing rooms before the riders go up to the Tower to start the run. I would need a great deal more than a beaker of this brew to even consider throwing myself, face first, down a vertical ice-sheet.

Whisk vodka, hot consommé, plenty of lemon juice, Worcester sauce and Tabasco in a blending machine.

ALEX'S MOROCCAN PREPRANDIAL

We drank copious quantities of this delicious cocktail before a September lunch in Marrakesh before dining on roasted grouse with all the traditional trimmings. They were shot by Nick and travelled out with us, courtesy of British Airways who are still none the wiser, stashed in the bottom of our suitcase in the hold - nice and cold. As with all proper drinks, this one tastes innocuous but packs a mean punch.

- Equal measures of sherry (fino or amontillado) and lemonade
- Lemon zest and lemon juice, to taste
- Plenty of mint leaves, finely chopped
- Ice

Mix all thoroughly in a large jug or pitcher and serve.

GIN, PROSECCO & ELDERFLOWER

Gin is enjoying a boom in popularity and now tops the list of trendiest spirits. Gin lovers thirst crazily for the galaxy of different makes and varieties, all with dazzlingly marketable names to add to their attraction, which have taken on the status of a prized and much sought after possession. I have a particular penchant for 'Silver Fox Gin'. Distilled five times, its purity and smoothness mean it tastes equally good 'on the rocks', as a traditional 'G & T' whilst also lending itself to a number of twists, such as this one, refreshingly good on summer days.

One shot each of gin and elderflower topped up with prosecco. Add a strip of cucumber or a sprig of mint or lemon verbena.

WHITE LADY

As far as real diehard cocktail imbibers go, this one should always be on the menu. This is guaranteed to make any party go with a swing and put fire in one's toes; but it's wise to bear in mind the Martini maxim here otherwise you will be both shaken and stirred.

"I like to drink martinis.
Two at the most.
Three I'm under the table
and four I'm under my host."

Pour equal measures of vodka and Cointreau into a glass. Add plenty of lemon juice mixed with the rind of the lemon and some citric acid. Shake this mixture up and leave it in the fridge for a week. Serve with plenty of ice. If it is too sweet, add more lemon juice, too bitter - a splash more Cointreau.

BLACK VELVET

All the poetic heft of Guinness coupled with Champagne. This was originally created by the bartender at Brooks's Club in London in 1861 to mourn the death of Queen Victoria's beloved husband, Prince Albert. Try toasting the seasonal return of oysters - when there is an 'r' in the month - with this, the finest of all oyster-washer-downers. It's a champion partner and also a welcome restorative if one is feeling jaded or just thoroughly hung-over.

Ideally, this should be drunk from a silver tankard half-filled with Champagne before pouring in the Guinness, over a spoon upside down, so that the beer will trickle down the inside of the glass and mix with the fizz below. You want to aim for the colour of pale mahogany.

BLACKBERRY WHISKY

Not strictly a cocktail but, nonetheless, good to have in the drinks cabinet. Make the most of the glut of autumnal blackberries to produce this popular brew for the sporting person's hip flask. Don't discard the alcohol steeped fruit once this is ready for drinking - use it in gravies and sauces to go with game or poured over ice-cream.

- Bottle of whisky - do buy a decent brand
- 2 kg / 4 lbs + blackberries
- 300g / 10 oz unrefined sugar

Pile the blackberries into a wide-necked, clean spirit bottle or large Kilner jar. Add the sugar and pour over the whisky. Seal tightly and leave for at least 2 months - turning from time to time to jiggle the sugar so that it dissolves.

SEA BREEZE

When the driver elect or a tea-total friend wants a change from elderflower cordial, this fits the bill well.

- Litre / 1 ¾ pint cranberry juice
- Juice of a lime
- Ice
- 400ml / ¾ pint grapefruit or orange juice

Mix all together and serve in a high ball glass.

GUNNER

Providing you use non-alcoholic ginger beer (look carefully when buying) you can have as many of these as you like 'for the road' with no ill effect.

Pour a can of cold ginger beer out, mix in freshly squeezed lime juice to taste plus a few shakes of Angostura bitters. Some also like to add ginger ale to this cocktail.

Picnics

Come rain or shine, there is nothing as quintessentially British as a picnic. Everything tastes better outdoors. This most carefree and leisurely style of entertaining appeals whether one is packing baskets for the beach (think of Sir John Betjeman's description of 'sand sandwiches'); riverside and boating regattas, operatic evenings, highland fairs and shooting picnics (where it is called a 'piece'), a day at the races or for a proper hike across moor and mountain. The secret of successful 'al fresco' is to ensure that the food is robust enough to withstand the rigours of transportation as well as any freak heatwaves.

LITTLE GEM SALAD BASKETS

Select robust leaves from Little Gem lettuces and arrange in a shallow dish fitting them snugly next to one another so they prop one another up and don't all collapse. Fill with any of the following ingredients:

- Peeled quail's eggs, halved
- Cherry tomatoes, halved
- Mozzarella, torn into pieces
- Basil leaves
- Anchovies
- Shelled prawns
- Rocket leaves
- Shelled broad beans
- Soft goat's cheese

Take Vinaigrette (page 211) or Tarragon Salad Sauce (page 219) in a jar and dress before serving.

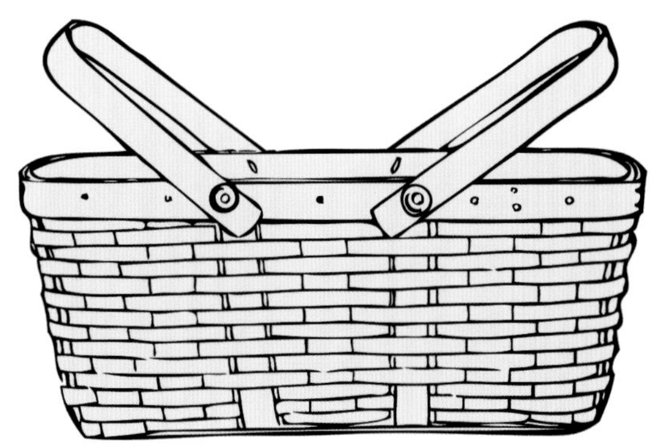

BOCADILLOS DE TORTILLA

I can remember the first time I had one of these as if it were yesterday. In fact, it was years ago having just got off the overnight ferry at Santander. I was starving and longing for breakfast. We stopped at a scruffy roadside café and the aromatic memories of this being cooked up on a tiny stove as well as its taste have stayed with me.

- 4 tbsp olive oil
- Onion, peeled and finely chopped
- 3 garlic cloves, peeled and finely diced
- 350g / 10 oz main crop potatoes, cooked, cooled and cut into small chunks
- 4 eggs, beaten
- Seasoning

Heat half the oil in a large non-stick frying pan and sauté the onion over a medium heat until totally soft and pale golden. Add the garlic and cook for a couple of minutes. Transfer to a bowl with the potatoes, eggs and mix together, seasoning well. Leave to stand for 20 minutes or so.

Heat the remaining oil in the frying pan and pour in the tortilla ingredients and cook over a medium heat until just set. Slide out of the pan and on to a plate, then put the pan on top and flip the tortilla back into it so that the uncooked side is facing downwards and fry again. Leave to cool until the tortilla has reached room temperature then cut into slices. Either eat with your fingers or split white bread rolls and fill with the tortilla.

OEUFS DRUMKILBO

(SERVES 6 - 8)

A great favourite of Her Majesty Queen Elizabeth, The Queen Mother - its fame has taken it into the cookery sections of both The Daily Telegraph and The Spectator. It also features in one of my favourite cookbooks 'A Taste of Mey'. This is really a designer prawn cocktail and egg mayonnaise all wrapped into one. It was supposedly first invented by Mrs Cruikshank, the 17th Lord Elphinstone's head cook at Drumkilbo. For me, it is the ultimate posh picnic food. Spoon the mixture into individual Kilner or jam jars and the job is done. No messing around with endless dishes or pots of mayo. Just provide everyone with a long handled spoon and they can eat away to their heart's content.

- 4 gelatine leaves
- 150ml / ¼ pint warm fish stock
- 450ml / ¾ pint mayonnaise, homemade ideally (page 216)
- 4 hard-boiled eggs, diced
- 250g / 8 oz prawns, cooked and shelled
- Meat from 2 lobsters
- 4 tomatoes, skinned, seeded and cut into quarters
- 6 drops Tabasco
- Tbsp tomato purée
- Juice ½ lemon juice
- Seasoning

Soak the gelatine leaves in a bowl of cold water for at least 10 minutes. Meanwhile heat the fish stock and when the gelatine is soft and pulpy, squeeze out the liquid and melt into the stock, then leave to cool. Place the mayonnaise in a bowl and add the fish stock/gelatine liquid. Add all the other ingredients to the mayonnaise and stir very gently to combine. Divide the mixture between the jars and chill to set.

To serve, top each one with a little mustard cress and a wedge of lemon and hand round with Fairy Toast (page 222).

EGG MOUSSE
(SERVES 8 FOR STARTERS, 4 AS A MAIN)

I have Janie Hall, an outstanding cook, gardener and friend, to thank for this timeless favourite which, when made properly, never loses its allure. Not only does it feature regularly for picnics and 'al fresco' eating, it should not be over-looked as a starter or lunch option.

- 6 hard-boiled eggs
- 5 - 6 sheets gelatine leaves
- Tbsp anchovy essence
- Few drops Worcester sauce
- 3 tbsp mayonnaise (if no homemade to hand, use a brand one)
- Tbsp tomato ketchup
- 300ml / ½ pint whipping cream, whipped to soft peaks
- Slug of sherry

Seafood Sauce:

To every 2 tbsp mayonnaise add the following:

- Tbsp tomato ketchup
- 2 tsp runny honey
- 2 drops Worcester sauce
- Pinch of paprika
- Shallot or ½ small onion, very finely chopped
- 6 - 8 tbsp double cream, whipped
- Seasoning

Mix all the ingredients for the seafood sauce carefully together.

For the mousse, ideally dice the egg whites minutely and rub the yolks through a sieve. If time is at a premium, however, then simply roughly chop the whole eggs very finely and put in a large bowl. Next, soak the gelatine leaves in a bowl of cold water for 10 minutes until soft. Add the anchovy essence, Worcester sauce, mayonnaise, tomato ketchup and the whipped cream to the eggs, mix thoroughly and season well. Squeeze the water from the gelatine leaves and put into a pan over a low heat with the sherry and stir until dissolved. Leave to cool slightly then mix into the egg mousse and combine thoroughly. Pour into a mould which has been rinsed out with cold water but not dried or into another suitable dish. Cover and refrigerate to set. Un-mould and decorate the centre of the egg mousse with washed watercress and serve with the sauce.

Tips FROM THE SINK

- As its name suggests, this sauce is also delicious with shellfish.

COURGETTE AND BASIL TART

Lionel and Judie Crisp's vegetable garden is a feast for the eyes. Better still, whenever I visit to ride my horse, they never fail to send me home with copious supplies of whatever is in season. Courgettes are that most summery of vegetables and nothing if not prolific. Here they are transformed into this handsome yet suitably rustic tart - fitting for every type of picnic as well as for lunches at home with a crisp green salad and plenty of crusty bread.

- 320g / 10 oz puff pastry
- Olive oil
- 2 garlic cloves, peeled and crushed
- 500g / 1 lb courgettes, trimmed and sliced
- 500g / 1 lb ricotta
- 100g / 4 oz Parmesan
- 4 eggs
- Handful basil leaves, roughly chopped
- Rasping freshly grated nutmeg
- Seasoning
- 50g / 2 oz pine nuts

Preheat the oven to 180 C. Roll out the puff pastry, prick all over and line a round or rectangular tin with it. Heat the oil in a large frying pan, add the garlic and sauté the courgettes until just coloured. Remove and drain on kitchen paper. In a bowl, mix together the ricotta with half the Parmesan, the eggs, basil and seasonings - don't worry if it looks a bit curdled at this stage. Cover the base of the dough with this and then put the courgettes on top and sprinkle on the remaining Parmesan. Bake in the oven for 20 minutes before scattering over the pine nuts then return to the heat for a further 10 minutes. Serve either warm or cold.

FUSILLI WITH COURGETTE, FETA AND BALSAMIC

I used to abhor the use of tupperware in general, not least for picnics, believing their sheer plasticity tainted the taste of the foods they stored. Nowadays, however, I am an ardent fan of those 'Lock & Lock' stackable airtight containers. Apart from anything else, there is no danger of the lid coming off. They are extremely versatile and excellent for salads such as this one.

- 400g / 14 oz fusilli
- 3 courgettes
- 6 tbsp olive oil, plus tbsp for drizzling
- 2 garlic cloves, peeled and thinly sliced
- 3 tbsp balsamic vinegar
- 4 mint sprigs, leaves picked and torn or finely sliced
- 100g / 4 oz feta, neatly cubed
- Black pepper

Cook the pasta until 'al dente' then run under cold water when draining to prevent it from continuing to cook. Cut the courgettes lengthways then slice into thin half-moon crescents. Heat the oil in the pan and fry the courgettes for a few minutes until golden, then add the garlic and splash with the balsamic vinegar and cook for a further minute. Take off the heat and add the feta and mint. Gently mix everything with a drizzle of olive oil and grind over the black pepper. This can be made 2 days before required and kept in the fridge.

PRESERVED LEMON CHICKEN

This dish fits with my style of cooking as it can be prepped in the morning (or even the day before) and left until you're ready to cook it. It's also great for supper with spinach and sautéed potatoes or scissored up once cooked and thrown into a salad with some bacon and avocado. You will find jars of preserved lemons on the supermarket shelves in the speciality foods section.

- 100g / 4 oz confit lemon flesh, pips removed
- Tbsp each of four of the following: parsley, tarragon, chives, basil and marjoram
- 2 tbsp olive oil
- Seasoning
- 4 chicken breasts or 8 boneless chicken thighs, beaten out

Take all the ingredients (bar the chicken) and place in a blender. Blitz until smooth. Rub the mix all over the chicken pieces, place them in the fridge and leave to marinate for a minimum of 2 hours. When ready, heat a heavy ridged pan until hot and simply griddle the escalopes (3 - 4 minutes on each side).

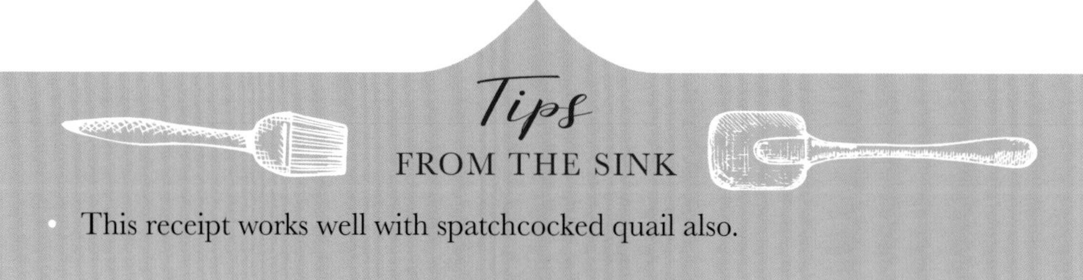

Tips
FROM THE SINK

- This receipt works well with spatchcocked quail also.

SHOW SAUSAGES

Over the years, these have become a regular feature of the picnic basket when we are off competing at shows and other equine events. Their virtue is that they taste good at any time of the day - for a predawn departure breakfast, mid-morning, at lunch or tea time or, should there be any left, on the homeward journey.

- 500g / 1 lb chipolata or cocktail sausages
- 2 tbsp maple syrup or runny honey
- Tbsp wholegrain mustard
- 2 tbsp sesame seeds

Preheat the oven to 180 C. Put the sausages into a baking tin. Mix together the syrup and mustard and pour over and cook for 15 - 20 minutes until nicely browned. Meanwhile, lightly toast the sesame seeds in a dry frying pan and scatter over the sausages.

POTATO SALAD

I like mine not too claggy. Opinions vary as to whether the potatoes should be peeled - I say not. Just well scrubbed. Some prefer theirs dressed with vinaigrette whilst others insist they should be smothered with mayonnaise. I like to use a mayonnaise/crème fraîche combination and, if I feel it is too thick, will run it down with a little milk. Capers, gherkins and / or thinly sliced radishes may all be added to the basic ingredients according to individual taste. Here is how I make mine.

- 500g / 1 lb Jersey Royals or waxy-fleshed salad potatoes - i.e. La Ratte
- 4 tbsp mayonnaise (preferably homemade (page 216) but a commercial brand is fine)
- 2 - 3 tbsp crème fraîche
- Milk, optional
- Bunch spring onions, ends and outer leaves removed, finely chopped
- 2 tbsp chives or chervil, finely scissored
- Seasoning

Cook the potatoes until done, drain and slice into neat chunks or rounds and leave aside to cool. In a separate bowl, combine the mayonnaise, crème fraîche, spring onions and herbs. Add a little milk if necessary so that the mayonnaise has a coating consistency and a little slackness to it. Taste to season. Turn the potatoes into this and mix all together thoroughly. Finish with more chives if wished.

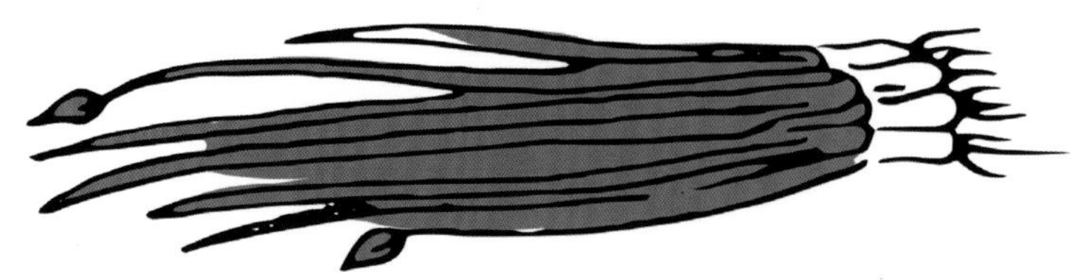

PENNY'S CHICKEN SANDWICH

Ever since the Earl of Sandwich, in need of sustenance, asked for some meat between two slices of bread in order to avoid disrupting a gambling game; the Sandwich has tended, for the most part, to summon up visions of blotting paper bread encasing plastic slices of ham and cheese, fart-smelling eggs, abrasive pickles and soggy lettuce spring to mind. The bin is the only place for such offerings. Happily, however, Penny's sarni is in another league. She tells me it was Chele Clarkin, mother of Jean-Paul - New Zealand's top international polo player - who introduced her to this. Full credit to the team!

- Proper white tin loaf of bread, crusts removed
- Cooked chicken, cut into strips
- Mayonnaise, Hellmann's is fine
- 2 tbsp celery or flat-leaf parsley leaves, finely chopped
- Bunch spring onions, white part only, trimmed and finely chopped
- Couple drops Tabasco
- Seasoning

Mix the chicken and other ingredients together then spread over the bread and make into sandwiches. Wrap well to keep fresh or store them under a damp tea towel.

As far as other recommendations for Sandwiches goes - remember, first of all, to experiment with different types of bread; i.e. sourdough, nutty brown bread, brioche or bridge rolls. Fillings include:

- Tomato with mozzarella and pesto
- Smoked ham and Cheddar with mustard mayonnaise
- Potted shrimps
- Smoked salmon, prawns and dill sauce
- Coronation chicken
- Fig, Parma ham and buratta
- Cucumber, Marmite and cream cheese
- Egg mayonnaise and cress

PRIZE-WINNING FLAPJACKS

These featured in ***Dishes With Dashers*** *but since then they have had a facelift. We never set off to one of our horsey events without a tin of these on board. Win or lose, these are always worthy of their own award.*

- 250g / 8oz butter
- 100g / 4 oz soft brown sugar
- 100g / 4 oz Demerara sugar
- Tbsp golden syrup
- Tbsp maple syrup
- Tbsp sea salt
- 450g / 12 oz porridge oats
- 2 large handfuls cornflakes

Preheat the oven to 160 C. Line a 20cm x 10 cm (9" x 5") or similar baking tray with greased parchment paper. Melt the butter, sugars and syrups and stir until the sugars have dissolved. Add the sea salt, mix well then tip in the porridge oats and cornflakes and stir thoroughly. Transfer to the tin and bake for approximately 12 - 15 minutes until the mixture begins to bubble and go golden brown. Remove from the heat and after 2 minutes, mark up into squares using a sharp knife. Allow to cool before lifting out and storing in a tin.

CHOCOLATE AND OLIVE OIL CAKE

Another receipt from Penny Lindsay-Fynn's bulging file of deliciousness which she has collected over the years. This is perfect for picnics and doubles up also as a handsome pudding when served with raspberries and a scoop of vanilla ice-cream. I can vouch for how well behaved it is - the first time I made it I forgot to add the egg yolks. The cake had gone into the oven and I was about to do the washing-up when I saw them sitting on the side. I hastily took the cake out of the oven and swirled them into the still liquid mixture. No-one ever knew. The end result possesses the density of a peat bog without being leaden. This is also gluten-free.

- 200g / 10 oz 70% dark chocolate, broken into squares
- 125ml / 4 fl oz olive oil
- 175g / 7 oz caster sugar
- 2 tbsp ground almonds
- Pinch of salt
- 5 eggs, separated

Preheat the oven to 180 C. Butter and line a 20 cm / 8" springform cake tin. Melt the chocolate in a bain-marie or alternatively put in a bowl and stand on the Aga top. When melted, pour in the oil in a steady stream then add ⅔ of the sugar, whisking all the time to dissolve. Remove from the heat and fold in the ground almonds, a pinch of salt and the egg yolks.

Beat the egg whites with the remaining sugar until you have firm peaks. Carefully fold in the chocolate mixture and then transfer to the prepared tin. Bake in the oven for 35 - 50 minutes. Test with a skewer to see that it is cooked. Remove from the heat and leave to cool in the tin - it will deflate and cracks will appear on the surface but this is all part and character of it. To serve, dust with icing sugar.

The Larder

The staple of every home has to be the larder or store cupboard. It is from within these shelves that the finishing touch to lunches, suppers and dinners emerge. The contents can also stand one in good stead when unexpected visitors arrive and impromptu lunches and suppers are necessary.

MY MA'S CHUTNEY

The trick with any chutney is to allow it sufficient time to mature. That way, the flavours can develop. This is always good with cold meats.

- 1 kg / 2.2 lbs peaches, skinned, stoned and sliced
- Onion, peeled and finely chopped
- 100g / 4 oz seedless raisins, soaked in boiling water until plump then drained
- Garlic clove
- Knob of root ginger, peeled and grated
- Tbsp mustard seed
- Cinnamon stick
- ¼ tsp cayenne pepper
- ½ tsp salt
- 600ml / 1 pint cider vinegar
- 500g / 1 lb soft brown sugar
- Apple, peeled, cored and minutely diced

Place all the ingredients in a large preserving (or similar) pan and cook over a low to medium heat until the mixture thickens. Transfer to sterilised pots, cover and seal and keep in a cool place.

RUNNER BEAN CHUTNEY

Newent Market, near Gloucester, takes place every Friday and it champions real food which is grown, produced and made by the wonderful local community. Everything is strictly seasonal here - asparagus, courgettes, soft buttery lettuces, summer fruits, copious bunches of heavenly scented sweet peas and so on. Come autumn, there are jars of this, my favourite chutney, which uses up the glut of those larger beans. As the saying goes, 'a fridge without chutney is like a car without a spare tyre'.

- 4 medium onions, peeled and diced
- 250ml / 12 fl oz malt vinegar
- 1kg / 2.2 lbs runner beans, strings removed and sliced on the diagonal
- Heaped tbsp English mustard powder
- Tbsp ground turmeric
- 25g / 1 oz cornflour
- 250ml / 12 fl oz white wine vinegar
- 250g / 8 oz granulated sugar
- 2 heaped tbsp wholegrain mustard
- 2 tsp flaked sea salt

Tip the diced onions into a large, heavy-based saucepan and pour over the malt vinegar. Bring to a gentle simmer, cover loosely and cook for 15 minutes until softened. Put the sliced beans into a large pan of boiling, salted water and return to the boil. Cook for 3 minutes then drain and refresh under cold water.

Mix the mustard powder, turmeric, cornflour and 4 tbsp of white wine vinegar until smooth. Stir the sugar and remaining white wine vinegar into the onion, bring to the boil and cook for 2 minutes. Add the beans and simmer gently for 10 minutes. Slowly pour the cornflour mixture into the onions and beans, stirring vigorously to dispel any lumps, followed by the wholegrain mustard and salt. Simmer for 20 minutes, stirring regularly so that the chutney does not catch and burn. Pot into warmed, sterilised jars and leave to cool. Cover, seal and label before storing in a dark place for at least a month.

SPICED PICKLED PEARS

There is a perfect time in the life of a pear when it's at peak ripeness. Indeed some gourmets go so far as to insist that you must, if necessary, be prepared to rise in the middle of the night to catch this precise moment. Luckily, though, pears need not always be so exacting as to be enjoyable. They are amenable to many different flavours lending themselves to both sweet and savoury flavours with cheese, wine and chocolate being the most common bedfellows. They also complement aniseed and therefore fennel; nuts such as walnuts, hazelnuts, pistachios and almonds plus caramel and cinnamon. Furthermore, they associate well with salad leaves such as watercress and chicory. When pickled they also go well with many cold meats including game and ham.

- 6 large firm pears (I use Comice)
- 500g / 1 lb sugar
- 250ml / 9 fl oz red or white wine vinegar
- Tsp whole cloves
- Tsp whole allspice
- Small piece of whole nutmeg
- Cinnamon stick

Peel, core and cut each pear into eight slices and place in a saucepan. Cover with approx 750ml / 1 ½ pints water. Boil briskly for 5 minutes. Strain off and reserve 600ml / 1 pint of the liquid and mix in the sugar, vinegar and spices. Pour over the pears and simmer until the pieces are cooked and translucent - approx 20 - 30 minutes. Pour into a bowl and leave overnight. Drain off the liquid the next day into a pan and boil hard to reduce it slightly. Pack the pears into a warmed sterilised Kilner jar with the spices and pour in the hot syrup to cover. Seal whilst warm and store for at least a month before use.

- Trussed up with some ribbon, this makes an original present for a foodie friend.

The Larder

CRANBERRY, PLUM AND STAR ANISE COMPÔTE

This lifts the classic cranberry sauce to a new level and is perfect for turkey, goose, ham and game dishes as well as terrines and don't forget a dollop inside a meaty sandwich too. It keeps well in a Kilner jar and also makes a good present. Can be frozen.

- 500g / 1lb fresh cranberries
- Punnet plums, stoned and roughly chopped
- 2 tbsp soft brown sugar
- Zest and juice of an orange
- Glass port or red wine
- 5 – 6 star anise
- Seasoning

Put all the ingredients into a saucepan and simmer on the heat so that the liquid reduces and the ingredients take on a jammy consistency. Taste to check seasoning/sweetness etc and, that's it.

Tips
FROM THE SINK

- Leftovers will also jazz up a pan of cooked red cabbage.

QUINCE JELLY

This chameleon-like fruit has magical qualities which are often long-forgotten and over-looked. Of all the orchard produce, it surely is the queen amongst fruits. Not only does it change colour in cooking but it immediately lifts and enhances a great many dishes including, amongst them, the most ordinary of apple pies raising its status to something altogether more exotic. Its hard, bullet-like appearance means it cannot be eaten straight from the tree and it must be cooked. Transformed into jams, jellies as well as quince paste to serve on the cheese board, it is surely well worth the effort involved. Try this jelly, which is so good alongside game.

- 8 - 10 quinces
- Handful of unripe windfall apples
- Unrefined sugar (500g / 1 lb to every ½ litre / pint of juice)
- 2 lemons

Make sure the jam jars are sterilised. Put a plate in the fridge for later use. Wash and quarter the fruit - no need to peel - and place in a large pan, cover with water and simmer until soft. Leave to cool then strain through a muslin cloth. Add 500g / 1 lb sugar for every pint of liquid. Using a potato peeler, strip the rind from the lemons in long lengths and tie up with a piece of string and plunge into the mixture. Juice the lemons and add to the liquid together with the sugar. Heat, stirring all the time, bring to the boil, skimming off the scum, and wait for setting point. To test, put a drop of the mixture onto the chilled plate, return to the fridge and after a couple of minutes, push with one finger. If the surface wrinkles, it is done. Remove the lemon rind and pot in sterilised jars.

CUMBERLAND SAUCE

Cumberland sauce is essential when serving ham and it is always a revelation to those who have never previously tasted a proper homemade version. It keeps indefinitely in the fridge and is brilliant with a whole variety of game as well as with meaty terrines. It need only ever be served at room temperature.

- 500g / 1 lb redcurrant jelly
- 3 oranges
- Lemon
- Large pinch ground ginger
- 3 tsp mustard powder
- Black pepper
- 350ml / 12 fl oz port

Put the redcurrant jelly in a pan on the heat to melt - I place the jar on top of the Aga. With a fine peeler, remove the skin of the oranges and lemon - you do not want to include the white pith. Halve the fruits and squeeze out the juice and reserve. Slice the skin to very thin slivers (julienne) and put in a little saucepan with some cold water and bring to the boil then simmer for 3 - 4 minutes and drain and refresh in cold water.

Put the blanched rinds, ginger and mustard powder plus the juice in a pan and let these simmer until the liquid is syrupy. Add freshly ground black pepper plus the port and reduce by half. Whisk in the melted redcurrant jelly and remove from the heat to cool.

Tips FROM THE SINK

- When cooking game, I often serve it with a jug of Cumberland sauce in place of gravy or another sauce.

STRAWBERRY, BALSAMIC AND BLACK PEPPER JAM

The great advantage of bounteous summer fruits is that there is enough to make one's own preserves and jams. Here, the strawberries should be unblemished and at their peak. If they are unripe they won't soften sufficiently and if they are over-ripe, then the fruit contains less pectin, colour and flavour. Smaller strawberries are always better as they retain their shape.

- 1.75kg / 4 lbs preserving sugar or sugar with pectin
- 1.75kg / 4 lbs strawberries, hulled
- Juice of 3 lemons
- Balsamic vinegar, to taste
- Black pepper

Preheat the oven to 110 C and set a plate in the fridge to chill. Thoroughly wash, rinse and drain the jam jars then place in the oven to sterilise them. Warm the sugar in a large ovenproof dish in the oven - I leave mine in a pan on top of the Aga. Place the strawberries and lemon juice in a preserving pan (or similar) and cook over a low heat for 6 - 8 minutes until the juices are running and the fruit is soft. Using a wooden spoon, stir in the warmed sugar until it dissolves. Add the balsamic vinegar and plenty of freshly ground black pepper. Bring to the boil, and cook quickly for about 10 - 15 minutes until the jam reaches setting point. To test, put a blob of jam on the cold plate from the fridge and chill for a few minutes. Gently push the jam with one finger and if the surface wrinkles then it has come to setting point. If it isn't ready, return the pan to the heat and continue boiling for a further few minutes, then repeat the test.

Once the jam has reached setting point, leave it off the heat to cool slightly, skimming the scum from the surface with a metal spoon and then stir in a nut of butter. Once the jam begins to cool, stir gently to distribute the fruit, then ladle or pour into the warmed jars and seal.

BOOZY PRUNES

Once steeped for at least a fortnight, these are a great larder staple to whip out as a last-minute pudding served alongside ice-cream, Greek yoghurt or Calvados cream (page 224).

- 200g / 7 oz muscavado sugar
- 200ml / 7 fl oz water infused with black tea
- Peel of a lemon
- Peel of an orange
- Vanilla pod, sliced lengthways
- 500g / 1 lb dried prunes, pitted
- Bottle of good Cognac or Armagnac

Boil the sugar and tea-infused water until the sugar has dissolved. Add the citrus peels and vanilla pod and bring back to the boil for a couple of minutes. Put the prunes into a bowl and pour over the syrup leaving to steep overnight. Remove the peel and vanilla pod and transfer the prunes and syrup into a sterilised jar. Pour in the Cognac or Armagnac and steep for at least two weeks.

Bits & Bobs

Odd receipts which don't immediately fall into one specific category but are far too good to omit.

RA'S SCRAMBLED EGGS

'Teaching your grandmother to suck eggs' may well be the reaction when readers see the inclusion of this most basic of receipts but it is surprising, nonetheless, how disappointing such a simple dish can be if the basic rules are ignored. Mediocre hotels are the worst sinners when they produce a pale and poor imitation having cooked the eggs until they have reached an almost concrete like consistency. RA had firm views on how to prepare this dish - well, indeed, he had fairly strong views on most matters - but he was well known for his delicious 'scramblers' as he called them. He insisted they should be cooked in a heavy-based frying pan and with a silver fork. I still use my old wooden spoon however, but thanks to him, I have exchanged saucepan for frying pan. Scrambled eggs should only ever be cooked to order - they do not improve for standing about!

- 75g / 3 oz butter
- 8 eggs
- A dash of milk or cream
- Seasoning

Using a fork, beat the eggs in a large bowl, add the milk and season very well. Heat a nut of the butter in a frying pan over a gentle heat until it forms a mild film but is not so hot it will brown. Pour in the eggs and with a wooden spoon, gently 'riddle' them round the pan stirring very slowly indeed so that they can start to cook. Add a few more nuts of butter and continue stirring so that they melt. As the eggs begin to gently scramble, draw the pan almost off the heat, add the last of the butter and stir again until a runny, creamy consistency is achieved. Remember that the eggs will continue to cook on a little once removed from the heat so take them off in time and pile onto pieces of toast. This does not require butter, there is more than enough in the eggs.

HERBED SEA SALT

Easily made using herbs from the garden. I pick rosemary, thyme, sage, mint and marjoram and tie it in bunches. Hang these up to dry for a few days. Mine go above the Aga but they could go in the airing cupboard. Next, strip the leaves from the stalks and stems, discarding the latter. Put 500g / 1 lb sea salt into the bowl of the food processor, add the herbs and blitz to blend to a coarse texture. Store in a jar and use when roasting chicken or potatoes or to sprinkle over vegetables when roasted or mashed avocados.

VINAIGRETTE

I make this in my food processor often doubling or even trebling the quantities in order to fill several bottles to have to hand.

- 2 tbsp red wine or sherry vinegar
- Tbsp Dijon mustard
- Seasoning
- Pinch caster sugar
- 200ml / 7 fl oz sunflower or groundnut oil
- 200ml / 7 fl oz olive oil
- Squeeze lemon juice

Put the vinegar, mustard, seasoning and sugar into the blender and blitz together. With the motor running, pour the sunflower/groundnut oil in through the funnel in a steady stream followed by the olive oil until they have homogenised. Add the lemon juice and a little water if too thick and then decant into a bottle.

- Keep your selection of oils at room temperature so that they combine more readily. I sometimes add some hazelnut or walnut oil to finish.

Bits & Bobs

BÉCHAMEL SAUCE

A speedy version of this classic white sauce. Do not, however, make the mistake of heating up the milk - if you do, then the effect of the hot liquid on the flour mean that those dreaded lumps will appear. And we want a velvet-smooth consistency.

- 50g / 2 oz butter
- 25g / 1 oz plain flour
- 25ml / ¾ pint cold milk
- Tsp English mustard
- Bay leaf
- Seasoning

Simply place all the ingredients in a saucepan over a medium heat and, using a balloon whisk, stir until the sauce starts to bubble and thicken. Turn down the heat and cook gently for at least 7 minutes.

This is the basic receipt - to this you may add a rasping of freshly grated nutmeg, white wine, cream and cheese.

GRAVY

Gravy is capable of dividing the nation since opinions differ as to what correctly defines gravy as opposed to a 'jus' or a sauce. The making of gravy in our family has always been a Sunday ritual based on the juices of the weekly roast joint. The fat is drained from the tin and then some flour is mixed in to form a roux before liquid is added. My mother always uses the water in which she has cooked the potatoes which she reserves when draining these. I have followed her example though stock is also a good alternative. To this I add my own curious cocktail of ingredients which include gravy browning, Bovril, tomato ketchup, redcurrant jelly, a good shake of the Worcester sauce bottle, a squeeze of lemon juice, some red wine (or port, Marsala, Madeira or sherry) and plenty of seasoning. It used to upset me that my Ma insisted on feeding the leftovers to her dogs. I freeze any leftover gravy, then add it to mince when I am making Shepherd's Pie (page 110).

To avoid confusion, those simple juices left in the pan after poultry, game or fish have been cooked are, strictly speaking, more of a jus.

CHICKEN STOCK

I can never bear to throw away a chicken carcass - in fact, I have even been known to ask for the remains of a poussin in a restaurant - hence my stockpot is permanently in use and the deep freeze always has a ready supply of stock. Should there not be an available carcass then I sometimes buy chicken wings instead. When it comes to what vegetables to add, I use whatever is to hand. Usually an onion or two (don't peel them though), the top and tail of leeks, carrots, mushroom stalks and/or tomatoes supplemented by bay leaves, parsley stalks and a handful of black peppercorns. The secret of making a great stock lies in throwing everything into a generously sized tin first and pouring on some olive oil then roasting in a hot oven until nicely coloured, approximately 25 minutes or so. Next, transfer to a large saucepan, cover with cold water and bring to the boil before simmering gently for several hours, topping up with water when necessary and skimming off any froth. Place a colander over a large bowl and pour the liquid through this leaving to stand for 15 minutes and pressing down well on the chicken and vegetables. Remove the colander and discard its contents and refrigerate the stock when cool. Remove the layer of fat which will have formed and strain again through a fine sieve. This will keep in the fridge for several days or can be frozen.

WILD GARLIC PESTO

That wonderful, whiffy foraged ingredient which cloaks the woods as spring gets underway makes an excellent pesto. Try it with my Kedgeree (page 57) or grilled lamb chops.

- 100g / 4 oz picked wild garlic leaves, stems removed
- 25g / 1 oz pine nuts, lightly toasted
- Garlic clove, peeled and crushed
- 200ml / 7 fl oz olive oil
- Zest of ½ lemon
- 25g / 1 oz Parmesan, finely grated
- Seasoning

Roll the leaves up tightly and slice thinly crossways. Put into the bowl of a food processor together with the pine nuts and garlic then, with the motor running, pour the olive oil in through the funnel. Stop the machine, add the lemon zest, cheese and seasoning and whizz again to blend. Transfer to a jar and store in the fridge.

AIOLI

Traditionally, this should be made in a pestle and mortar - but a bowl and whisk work equally well as does a food processor. In France it is often served alongside a dish of mixed crudités. I like it with plain poached or grilled chicken and, of course, Bouillabaise (pages 74).

- 2 egg yolks
- 2 garlic cloves, peeled and crushed
- Seasoning
- 300 - 450 ml / ½ - ¾ pint olive oil
- Juice of a lemon

Beat the yolks together with the garlic and a pinch of sea salt until thick. Add the oil in a very thin trickle, beating continuously. Pour in a little of the lemon juice and then some more oil. Continue beating, adding more lemon juice and oil alternately until both have been used up and the mayonnaise has thickened. Check the seasoning and cover and chill until required. Bring to room temperature before serving.

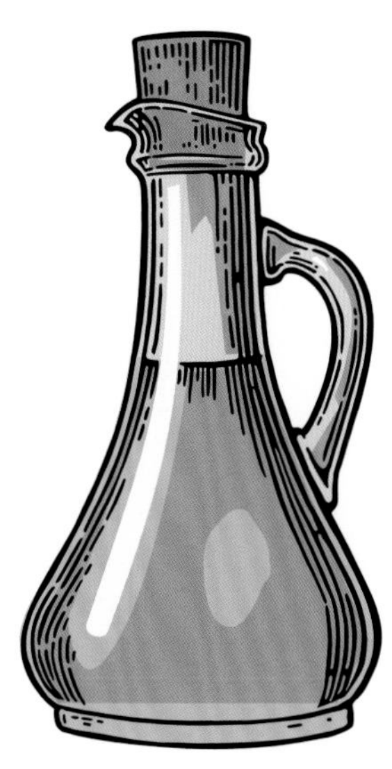

FAST MAYONNAISE

We have all been taught how to make mayonnaise by dutifully whisking together two egg yolks with Dijon mustard and then slowly trickling in the oil until the mixture begins to thicken and emulsify. Satisfying but somewhat slow. This version is quickly whipped up and takes no time at all. Keep a jar to hand in the fridge. If it is a herby mayonnaise you are after, then blend in the herbs at the end and watch it turn a lovely fresh, bright green.

- 2 eggs
- 300ml / 10 fl oz groundnut oil
- 200ml / 7 fl oz olive oil
- Splash white wine vinegar
- Seasoning
- Squeeze lemon juice
- (Handful fresh herbs, leaves only, i.e. parsley, tarragon, chives, sorrel, basil)

Put the eggs into the bowl of a food processor and slowly pour in the groundnut oil until it emulsifies. Add the olive oil and the white wine vinegar and blend again. Season and add a squeeze of lemon juice if necessary.

CARPACCIO SAUCE

Carpaccio is named after Vittoire Carpaccio, the Venetian Renaissance painter known for his brilliant use of reds and whites in the minute detail of his infinite perspective landscapes. It was invented by hotelier Giuseppe Cipiani of Harry's Bar fame where it has always ranked high amongst the many delicious dishes on their menu. When serving this sauce on the Carpaccio, it helps to use a squeeze bottle to create Jackson Pollock-esque streaks for which this dish is so widely celebrated.

- 350ml / ⅓ pint homemade mayonnaise (page 216)
- 1 - 2 tsp Worcester sauce
- Tsp lemon juice
- 2 - 3 tbsp milk
- Salt and freshly ground white pepper

Put the mayonnaise into a bowl, add the Worcester sauce (to taste) and lemon juice then run down with the milk to achieve a sauce-like consistency. Season well and transfer to a squeeze bottle before decorating the meat.

SALSA VERDE

An ace accompaniment to grilled chicken and fish; or to go with pasta dishes, vegetables and salads. A tub in the fridge will mean you are never short of a sauce.

- 2 tbsp each flat-leaf parsley and mint leaves, roughly chopped
- 3 tbsp capers, drained and rinsed
- Small tin anchovy fillets, drained
- Garlic clove, crushed
- Tsp Dijon mustard
- Juice of ½ lemon
- 125ml / 4 fl oz olive oil
- Sea salt

Pile the parsley, mint, capers and anchovies onto a chopping board and grind to a coarse paste, or do so using a pestle and mortar. If using a board, transfer these ingredients to a bowl then stir in the mustard, lemon juice, olive oil and salt. Transfer to a clean jar or tub and store in the fridge.

TOMATO SALSA

I love this alongside my Kedgeree (page 57). Alternatively, use it as a topping for bruschetta and, if wished, substitute the coriander for basil.

- 500g / 1lb vine plum tomatoes, skinned (page 228)
- Bunch spring onions, white part only, finely sliced crossways
- Tbsp coriander leaves
- Juice ½ lemon
- 3 tbsp olive oil
- Tbsp sesame oil

Chop the tomato flesh very finely, discarding the seeds and mix with the spring onions. Mix in the coriander, lemon juice and oils and season to taste. Store in jar in the fridge.

TARRAGON CREAM SAUCE (HOT)

Some people regard this as an overworked cliché in the kitchen; as if it has been done to death. I don't care - I simply love it and after all, tarragon and a fine chook are one of those culinary marriages which just works. Make in advance then reheat before serving.

- 300 ml / ½ pint jellied chicken stock (page 213)
- Splash Noilly Prat or white wine
- 3 tbsp double cream
- Squeeze lemon juice
- 2 tbsp tarragon leaves, chopped
- Seasoning

Put the chicken stock into a saucepan and bring to the boil, then lower the heat and reduce the liquid by half before adding the Noilly Prat or white wine. Pour in the cream and whisk well then the lemon juice and tarragon. Season to taste.

TARRAGON SALAD SAUCE (COLD)

This one lends itself not only to cooked chicken but also to salads, cold poached salmon, hard-boiled eggs as well as alongside vegetable crudités.

- 150 ml / 4 fl oz mayonnaise
- ½ tsp English mustard
- Tbsp tarragon or white wine vinegar
- 3 tbsp single cream
- 3 tbsp tarragon leaves, chopped
- Pinch caster sugar
- Seasoning

Mix all the ingredients together.

MAGGIE'S ASPARAGUS SAUCE
(SERVES 6)

Melted butter, Hollandaise and vinaigrette are common place partners to seasonal spears. Try this one for a change, given to me by Maggie Heath.

- 250g / 8 oz butter
- Tbsp Dijon mustard
- Grated zest and juice of an orange and a lemon
- Tabasco
- Seasoning

Put all the ingredients into a pan, melt the butter and whisk well. Serve warm.

BREAD SAUCE

Essential to serve with roasted chicken and game.

- 6 whole cloves
- Onion, skin removed
- 450 ml / ¾ pint milk
- Bay leaf
- 6 whole peppercorns
- 75g / 3 oz day-old white breadcrumbs
- 2 tbsp butter
- Seasoning
- 2 tbsp double cream

Stick the cloves into the onion. Put the milk into a saucepan and add the onion, bay leaf and peppercorns. Simmer gently for 15 minutes and leave to infuse for an hour.

Put the breadcrumbs into another saucepan, strain the milk over them, add the butter and seasoning and cook over a gentle heat for 15 minutes, stirring occasionally. Add the cream, check the seasoning and serve in a sauceboat.

GLAZE FOR BAKED HAM

Ok, so perhaps I cheat a little when it comes to cooking the Yuletide ham, centrepiece of the Christmas table, as my butcher cooks mine for me. Ask your butcher to do likewise and to rip off the rind leaving you with a good covering of fat.

- 3 tbsp marmalade
- 3 tbsp brown sugar
- 2 tbsp black treacle
- 2 tbsp pomegranate molasses
- Zest of an orange

Preheat the oven to 190 C. Mix all the ingredients together in a bowl. Score this and stud the point of each diamond with whole cloves and sit in a roasting tin then pour over the ham and cook in a hot oven for 15 - 20 minutes maximum, basting two or three times, until just browned and glistening. Serve either hot or cold with Cumberland Sauce (page 206).

PICKLED CUCUMBER

Cucumbers are often blamed for giving people indigestion. Treated in this way, any hint of such a complaint will be dispelled.

- Large cucumber, peeled and very thinly sliced
- Tbsp caster sugar
- Tbsp dill leaves, chopped
- ¼ glass white wine vinegar
- Sea salt

Put the cucumber into a large flat dish, sprinkle over the sugar, dill, white wine vinegar and season with salt. Place saucers on top to cover and weight these with either old fashioned kitchen scale lead weights or cans of beans or similar. Put in the fridge for at least half an hour then remove the weights and drain off the liquid (more will have accumulated from the cucumber juices) and hand round in a small bowl.

FAIRY TOAST

Strictly speaking, this is Melba toast but I have always called it Fairy Toast on account of its delicate appearance.

- 8 slices white bread

Preheat the grill, if you have one. I don't so I use the top oven of the Aga and keep the door ajar. Start by toasting the bread in the toaster, turned down to a low heat, until just starting to colour. Remove immediately and cut off the crusts then slide a serrated knife horizontally through the middle to produce two thinner slices. Discard any 'doughy' lumps. Don't allow the toast to get cold otherwise it won't work. Place the pieces either under the grill, cut sides uppermost or on a tray in the Aga. Watch carefully - they should curl and crisp up but not burn. Store in a tin if making ahead.

COGNAC BAKED BRIE
(SERVES 8 - 10)

This unctuous dish comes from Karl Baston who learnt his trade at the Michelin-starred and thus appropriately named Star Inn, at Harome in Yorkshire. Karl brought his own skills to the Cotswolds some years ago and is now chef at The Mount Inn near Broadway.

- 150g / 6 oz light muscovado sugar
- 200g / 7 oz walnuts, finely chopped
- 900g / 1 ¾ lb wheel of Brie
- 125ml / ¼ cup Cognac

In a small bowl, mix the sugar, walnuts and brandy. Place the Brie on a roasting tray, lined with parchment (or similar paper) and spoon the walnut mixture on top, covering it completely. Wrap the Brie (on its tray) in cling film and refrigerate for a good couple of hours.

Preheat the oven to 200 C, unwrap the cheese and bake for 10 - 15 minutes, until it starts to melt. Allow to cool a little before serving with Fairy Toast (page 222) or crackers.

CUSTARD

As a child, those vivid red, blue and yellow tins of Bird's Eye custard powder were a source of amazement to me. Never mind the fact that it was an egg-free imitation of the real thing, I regarded it as nothing short of miraculous that just as milk was added to this concoction then hey presto, the next thing one knew the jug of custard was on the table. Here is how to make your own from scratch - incomparably nicer and a great deal healthier!

- Vanilla pod
- 300 ml / ½ pint double cream
- 3 egg yolks
- Tbsp caster sugar
- Tsp cornflour

Split the vanilla pod lengthways and scrape out the seeds. Put these into a saucepan together with the cream and bring up to boiling point. In the meantime, beat the egg yolks, sugar and cornflour together in a small bowl. Pour the hot cream in, stirring continuously, and return the mixture to the saucepan. Heat very gently, still stirring, until the sauce has thickened. Do not be tempted to cook this over anything other than a low heat otherwise it may get too hot and start to look granular.

CALVADOS CREAM

- 300ml / ½ pint double cream
- 2 tbsp icing sugar, sieved
- Generous tot (or three) of Calvados or brandy

Whip the cream until it forms soft peaks then fold in the icing sugar and alcohol. Refrigerate until required.

RASPBERRY SAUCE

Wonderful with ice-creams, Summer Pudding (page 140) and the Velvet Chocolate Torte (page 154).

- 400g / 14 oz raspberries
- Juice of an orange
- 100 ml / 3 ½ fl oz red wine
- Sugar, to taste

Put the fruit, orange juice and red wine into a saucepan and heat through gently just until the raspberries begin to disintegrate. Taste to see whether it needs any sugar and add accordingly. Purée then pass through a sieve and store in a jar in the fridge.

SUGAR SYRUP

- 300g / 10 oz granulated sugar
- 200ml / 7 fl oz water
- Glass white wine
- Strips of lemon, lime or orange peel, pith removed

Whisk all the ingredients together in a pan over a gentle heat and simmer, stirring to dissolve the sugar, for 8 - 10 minutes. Cool, strain and pour into a screw top jar or bottle. Keep in the fridge and use as required.

Techniques

Basic methods which tend to come up time and again within receipts as useful reference points.

HOW TO SHUCK OYSTERS

Oysters are alive until shucked so, like mussels, discard any that are already open. Place oysters in the fridge until you are ready to prepare them, preferably on ice. A fishmonger will be able to provide you with a large quantity of crushed ice for storing and presentation.

To shuck, clean each oyster with a stiff scrubbing brush under cold running water. Hold the oyster with a tea towel or damp dishcloth for good purchase and keep the flat shell on the top, prising the oyster open by twisting your shucking knife into the hinge until you get an opening. Working swiftly so that it doesn't close up again, run the knife along the inside of the top shell to cut the muscle and take off the flat shell, ensuring the oyster is steady in order to retain the juices. Lastly, loosen the oyster from the bottom shell. Once shucked, serve the oysters or prepare them as for Fred's Bloody Oysters (page 48).

HOW TO SKIN TOMATOES

A simple task but again, it makes all the difference to the end result of so many tomato dishes when this fruit has to stand on its own merits.

Fill a bowl with ice and water and another with boiling water. Remove any stems from the tomatoes and drop them into the boiling water and watch their skins begin to wrinkle - about 50 seconds. If they show no signs of doing so, prick them with the end of a sharp knife. Scoop out with a slotted spoon and transfer to the ice bath. Once cooled, lift out onto the chopping board. Peel off the skins and either cut into quarters and seed or simply slice.

HOW TO ROAST & SKIN PEPPERS

The transformation effected by the simple action of direct heat produces the most gloriously silken sweet, seductive and woody overtones which is usually a revelation to those whose views on peppers is a 'take it or leave it' vegetable.

The basic technique is to char the skin of the pepper all over without cooking the flesh beyond a certain stage of softness. The most effective way to achieve this is to grill them under the hottest of preheated grills turning each side as they are done. If, like me, you are grill-free, sit them on a baking sheet and place in a very hot oven then stand close by, fork in hand, to supervise blistering them all over.

The peeling is a messy old business and must be done whilst they are still hot. Scrape away the skin with a knife and cut out the stem and seeds and throw these away. Rinse off the debris briefly under a cold tap but don't linger or you wash away much of the flavour. Cut into halves or thin strips and proceed, accordingly, with your receipt.

CLARIFIED BUTTER

As butter is an emulsion, it is great as it is for sauces but requires clarifying should you want to use it as a preservative. You need it to get just enough heat to evaporate the water but not too much heat that it burns.

Melt butter in a saucepan over a medium-low heat until it foams after around 8 - 10 minutes and then, just as dark flecks start to appear, remove from the heat and strain through a muslin or kitchen paper lining a sieve into a jug or bowl, taking care not to tip any residue watery liquid into this vessel.

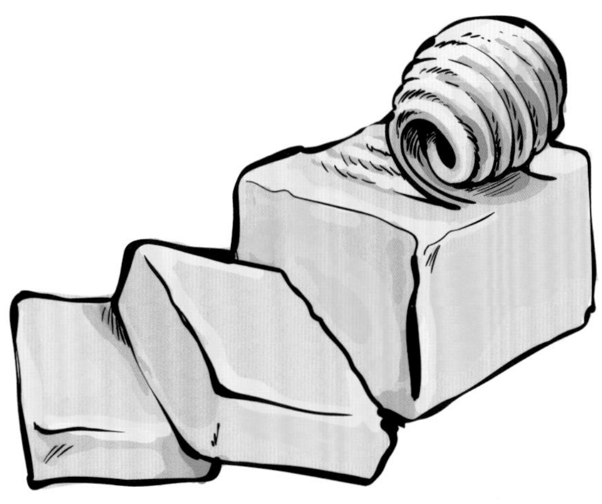

Dashers

Index

Index

Index

Index

Index